CW00376475

Contemporary Poems:
Some Critical Approaches

Contemporary Poems: Some Critical Approaches

edited by
Lesley Jeffries and Peter Sansom

Smith/Doorstop Books

Published 2000 by
Smith/Doorstop Books
The Poetry Business
The Studio
Byram Arcade
Westgate
Huddersfield HD1 1ND

ISBN 1-902382-26-9
British Library Cataloguing-in-Publication Data. A catalogue record
for this book is available from the British Library.

Printed by Bath Press Limited, Bath

Smith/Doorstop Books are represented by Signature Book
Representation Ltd, 2 Little Peter Street, Manchester M15 4PS, and
distributed by Littlehampton Book Services Ltd.
The Poetry Business gratefully acknowledges the help of Kirklees
Metropolitan Council and Yorkshire Arts.

ACKNOWLEDGEMENTS

The editors and contributors would like to thank all the following for granting
copyright permission:
Bloodaxe Books for two poems from *Zoom!* by Simon Armitage, published 1989
Carcanet Press Ltd, for poems and extracts from *New and Collected Poems* by Edwin
Morgan, from *Collected Poems* and *Five Fields* by Gillian Clarke, and from *Selected
Poems* by Ian McMillan
Faber & Faber, for poems and extracts from *The Spirit Level* by Seamus Heaney,
from *Kid* by Simon Armitage, and from *Birthday Letters* by Ted Hughes.
Tony Harrison, for an extract from 'Illuminations', *Selected Poems*, 1987
Peterloo Poets for poems and extracts from *Consequences, Side Effects, Standing To,
Safe as Houses, A Watching Brief* and *Voices Off,* by U.A. Fanthorpe

CONTENTS

PREFACE

We'd originally thought of this book as a series of essays on contemporary poetry, each one from a different critical perspective. Exemplifying theory soon became less interesting to us, though, than getting to grips with the work – with poems, that is, rather than poets, in whichever way best suited the critic and the text.

Nevertheless, each essay makes its angle of approach clear, and in her introduction Lesley Jeffries provides a description of these approaches in the context of the book overall. The introduction also identifies surprising similarities between at first sight dissimilar undertakings, and this may be why the book seems more coherent to us than we once feared.

With the exception of Martin Dodsworth's piece (taken from a recent Thom Gunn issue of *Agenda*), all of the essays were commissioned. And, though Lesley and I made suggestions and explained our rough ground plan, within this the writers were invited to make their own choice of poet as well as treatment.

I should say that there are other poets we'd hoped to bring into the debate – it may be invidious to name names, but certainly David Constantine and Vicki Feaver spring to mind, among many others. For a moment or two we considered widening the catchment overseas, to include, for instance, Sujata Bhatt and Les Murray, but this would have made the book unwieldy. But then, there's always the next volume …

Peter Sansom

INTRODUCTION

This volume of essays opens with a discussion by Ray Mackay of the language used by **Seamus Heaney** in *The Spirit Level*. The essay has two aspects that I think are worthy of mention here. First, Mackay sets out his approach, which he labels 'subjective stylistics'. Although there has been a heated debate recently about the objectivity or otherwise of stylistics, the term 'subjective stylistics' is not yet widely used, and readers might like to ponder their own response to this debate. Mackay places himself at one 'extreme' by his statement that 'There can be no set of objective criteria against which to measure these judgements because there can be nothing which is not interpreted by the individual'. He also claims to be doing nothing more than 'trying to change the way you read'. My own personal view is that the extreme Mackay adopts is unnecessarily severe and is belied by his own practice. Whilst there may well be differing, and sometimes conflicting, interpretations of any text, particularly poetry, the whole basis of linguistic communication depends for its success on there being at least some agreement as to how the whole system works. Thus, there will potentially be at least some agreement as to the meaning of any text, at least to the extent that some interpretations may be 'wrong'. Bringing forward evidence, based on a joint (though constantly shifting) understanding of how language works, seems to me a *relatively* objective exercise. Mackay would, of course, disagree. At the other extreme, most stylisticians would at least agree that their enterprise is not *absolutely* objective. I believe that many scientists would hold a similar view about their own practices.

The second aspect of Mackay's essay that should be mentioned is the very convincing case that he presents to reconcile two apparently opposing views of the poems in *The Spirit Level*. Critics have described the poems as 'light' ('airy, buoyant') and 'heavy' ('sombre', 'self-burdening'). Mackay deftly shows how these tendencies are both present in the language of the poems, with reference to their lexis, locatives, imagery and form. The use of these particular headings reflects a stylistic practice which owes more to literary critical than to linguistic traditions. This does not invalidate the approach, indeed, it may be a more accessible practice for students unfamiliar with the more technical descriptions produced by linguistic approaches (see Chapter 3 for an example). The difference between these approaches might be exemplified by the analysis of lexis, where Mackay's discussions often point to presumed self-evident meanings of individual words (such as the heaviness of 'ox') rather than to other, more general characteristics, such as a particular kind of oppositeness, or the presence of polysemy. Mackay's approach does, however, reflect some linguistic influences, such as when he uses grammatical structure, in the form of prepositional phrases, to investigate the 'groundedness' of the poems.

The second chapter, on the poetry of **Tony Harrison**, addresses a criticism that is often made of his poetry; that he uses cliché too often and to little effect. Geoff Hall's essay is informed by a range of literary and linguistic theories and practices, but perhaps most importantly by Bakhtin on the one hand and Conversational Analysis on the other. Hall's contention is that far from using cliché as a lazy or uncreative form of language, particularly in Harrison's early collection entitled *The School for Eloquence*, the poet has both a polemical and an artistic reason for using cliché judiciously.

The early part of the essay argues that accessibility and anti-elitism are part of Harrison's project; 'a deliberately provocative gesture of solidarity with the culture of his background'. Hall claims that the use of the everyday expression, particularly cliché, was anathema to modernism and that Harrison's use of cliché is a reaction to this view. Hall sets up an apparent opposition whereby the 'Romantic' view of literary purpose is to 'make new', using new language, whereas everyday language, including cliché, is by its nature repetitive and 'dead'. He then proceeds to dismantle this opposition, concluding by the end of the essay that Harrison achieves the apparently impossible feat of making over-familiar language live anew for the reader.

On his way to this conclusion, Hall uses evidence from conversational analysis to demonstrate convincingly that the purpose of Harrison's use of cliché is both to 'close' the topic of a poem, and to indicate the emotional importance of the issues under discussion. These effects both reflect the common use of cliché in everyday life, such as when people are trying to finish a tricky conversation where there is a fundamental disagreement or where something uncomfortable like a death has been discussed. One of the useful aspects of cliché, Hall argues, is that because they are often metaphorical, it is not easy to disagree with them. They therefore make perfect 'closing' remarks. An incidental bonus of Hall's essay is the explanation of the genesis of cliché, both etymologically and conceptually, from the rise of mass printing and literacy.

The stylistic approach I take in Chapter 3 uses 'deixis' as an analytical tool to explore the worlds created in **Carol Ann Duffy**'s poems, and how they seem to draw the reader into their centre. The concepts of deixis, familiar to some but not all readers, are explained, so that the essay can draw on the distinction between close-up time, place and person ('now', 'here' and 'I') and distanced time, place and person ('then', 'there' and 'you' or 's/he'). The essay argues that irrespective of whether Duffy is writing in her 'own' or someone else's voice, whether or not she has an explicit addressee and whether or not that addressee is clearly the reader or someone else, the poems manage to draw readers in by placing them at the poem's focal point.

The three sections, dealing with place, time and person respectively, each demonstrate Duffy's use of deictic words, such as 'here' and 'now', to give a particular 'point of view' in each poem. They also show how the differences between 'here' and 'there', 'now' and 'then', 'you' and 'me' are sometimes blurred, to reflect the uncertainties of people's lives, whether it is because they are displaced from their home or far from a loved one. This essay combines a technical analysis with literary responses to the poems. This seems to me rather similar in practice to Mackay's earlier chapter on Heaney, though I would not want to label my analysis entirely 'subjective'. One of the things it does not do, unlike Hall, but in common with Mackay, is make judgements about the literary merit or otherwise of the poems themselves, though in fact I hope my regard for Duffy's poetry is implicit. Stylistics tends not to make judgements, and may use its techniques to look at any text, literary or not, irrespective of cultural 'worth'. As we will see, the essays written from a more literary, or writerly, perspective, are much readier to make such judgements.

The essay on **Thom Gunn**'s poem, 'The Hug', by Martin Dodsworth, is a case in point. From the first paragraph he makes it clear that he wants to argue for the poem's excellence, and every point he makes is framed in terms that praise its achievement. The techniques used by Dodsworth are a combination of textual and intertextual references, though he doesn't use this latter term explicitly. Dodsworth refers to formal features such as rhyme and line length as well as individual words and the structure of the final sentence. A stylistician could have made very similar points, and would have spent longer explaining 'how' the effects are achieved – and in more technical language! Here, readers are given the conclusions and left with a 'gap' to fill in regarding the way in which these effects are reached. This is a literary, rather than an analytical technique, though the evidence is all there. The intertextuality comes in the form of a number of references to seventeenth century and even sixteenth century literature. Dodsworth points out what he calls 'an obvious allusion' to Donne's 'The Extasie' as well as making comparisons with the work of Herbert, Herrick and Ben Jonson, 'whose work Gunn specially admires'. We are not given evidence of this latter assertion, though it is said with great confidence, and we are persuaded to believe it!

Dodsworth's case for this poem depends on such intertextual references, as well as other knowledge about Gunn himself. The poem is a celebration of a relationship, and the knowledge that it is a gay relationship is both vital to the case Dodsworth is making, and also necessarily not textual. In fact, there is a case, that Dodsworth makes, for the word 'chest' being an indication of a male rather than a female lover, but his main point concerns the irrelevance of the sex – and sexuality – of the partners. Gunn, he claims, is putting gay love into a context, including the Metaphysical Poets' work, where heterosexual love has long been celebrated. He is 'normalising' the experience, particularly by the use of the word 'familial', to rejoice in the relationship – any relationship – that puts an end to the ultimate isolation of the human condition.

Peter Sansom's own contribution to this volume comes in the form of an appreciation of **Simon Armitage**'s poems, three in particular, from a writer's perspective. It represents the most 'writerly' end of our spectrum here, though it also has resonances for stylisticians and critics. Indeed, Sansom explicitly addresses the overlap in interests when he states that wide reading and close reading of poetry are essential to good practice in composition. Whilst he endorses some general principles of poetic writing, such as organicism ('poem as exploration or act of discovery'), Sansom also shows that the analysis of poems can be rewarding for the writer, though his analysis stops short of the technical description you'd expect of more academic approaches. This is illustrated by phrases such as 'unforced rightness of the diction' and 'accurate but surprising to say a "set of ripples"'. In these cases a different approach might want some explanation of why the diction is 'right' and might call the second an instance of unusual collocation. As Sansom says, he is trying to explain 'not what the poet has achieved, but why'.

The other freedom which a writer's approach allows you is the luxury of judgement. Sansom feels free to talk about the '*lovely* half-rhyme, "inertia" and "water"' and to berate Dr Freud who 'might come in with his big boots, diagnosing something sinister, and he'd be wrong', though he also indicates where a more analytical approach would go next: 'or else the poem would be more explicit elsewhere'. Like Dodsworth, Sansom indicates other approaches in his own. He refers to some of Armitage's 'allusions', which would be labelled intertextuality in other approaches. He calls what he is doing 'a sort of layman's stylistics'. In general, though, his article tries to use the close analysis of poems to demonstrate that what marks Armitage out as a poet is his ability to get the literal detail right, whilst allowing 'the figurative to speak through it'.

In Ian Gregson's chapter on **McMillan**, **Hattersley** and **Duffy**, he draws parallels between these three poets, as well as with other writers from a range of periods, to demonstrate his thesis that they all draw on the caricatural tradition as well as incorporating a postmodern outlook into their work. He uses a mainly thematic discussion of the poems to illustrate the point that 'these caricatural images intersect with postmodern anxieties about the self because they question the boundaries of the human.' Gregson's approach is one of trying to trace the historical (and to a certain extent also geographical) context in which the three poets are writing. He refers to the twentieth century continuation of the use of caricature, found in popular culture as well as literature, from Monty Python to South Park.

The themes he finds all share a fascination with disassembled human bodies, and/or humans as machines or animals, that are to be found in both the satirical tradition of caricature and magic realism. Gregson proposes that these traditions and surrealism all encompass, though not always explicitly and sometimes prior to its naming, the concepts of 'postmodernism'. Although he refers to a number of extracts, and gets close to Sansom's kind of 'lay' stylistic analysis at times, most of Gregson's concern is with the imagery. To the extent that it concerns language at all, he describes in broad brush strokes, for example, McMillan's tendency to mingle 'diverse genres and registers'.

Gregson shares with Sansom a desire to discover what Sansom calls the 'impulse' behind the writing, though he does not write here from a writer's but rather from an academic's point of view. Though it is implicit that he values the poetry he is discussing, his aim is not to elucidate what it is that bestows that value on the poems, but rather how they fit into his understanding of their literary and personal context. One of the techniques used in work like Gregson's is the use of further similes and metaphors to throw light on the imagery of the writing under consideration. For example, in a discussion of Duffy's poem 'Standing Female Nude', he uses the image of the Russian doll to describe the different 'consciousnesses' at work in the poem.

One of Gregson's observations about McMillan, Hattersley and Duffy is that they all take on the postmodern concern with the lack of stability of human personality and identity. This is echoed in Diane Davies' chapter on notions of identity in the poetry of **Gillian Clarke**, whose recognition as a female poet working in the Anglo-Welsh tradition gives her both nation and gender as points of potential conflict in her identity. Davies combines psychoanalytic and feminist theory with stylistic analysis to draw conclusions about Clarke's themes of rootedness and fluidity in the issues of nationhood and gender. She uses the categories of linguistic deixis to demonstrate that Clarke blurs boundaries of selfhood and otherness, time and space. This is an argument that parallels the one in my earlier chapter on Duffy. Both poets, then, seem to want to challenge the historical certainties that they have inherited, and in the case of Clarke, Davies claims that this is achieved with more than a glance backward to the female tradition, with all its restrictions, of her country.

Davies combines theoretical ideas of the Imaginary (from Lacan) and the Symbolic (from Kristeva) with deixis, to propose that the breakdown in 'normal' linguistic usage that she observes in Clarke's work is a symptom of the semiotic (or anarchic) stage that children go through before they enter the Symbolic (i.e. before learning language). Some claim that women remain more able than men to access this 'pre-linguistic' sensibility, and though Davies acknowledges the capacity for male poets to similarly get behind the conventional, she implies that Clarke is particularly adept at this accessing of the imagination. Davies' approach is explicitly to combine the literary and the linguistic in analysing poetry, with the claim that this is more enlightening than either on their own.

In the following chapter, Paul Mills writes about **Edwin Morgan**'s poems from a literary perspective, and with few exceptions taking the language as to some extent transparent, rather than using stylistic or textual analysis to 'uncover' meanings. This is not to say that Mills ignores the poems, every point he makes is illustrated from them, and he builds a picture of Morgan as a creator of worlds ('textworlds' as some would call them), but significantly of worlds where the reader is invited to make their own contribution to the meaning of the poem. Whilst Morgan's poems do not drum home any obvious messages, Mills observes that they are not entirely free of attitude. They present the reader with situations, often with dramatic events, but also with a range of voices, and frequently including a bewildered voice that undermines other certainties.

One of the informing theories of Mills' work, although it is not made explicit, is 'The Death of the Author'. Mills makes it clear that although he is anxious to get at what the poems 'might' mean, the reader is free to make a range of meanings from Morgan's poems. The paradox is that Mills also claims it is Morgan himself that allows the reader such freedom, almost implying that the presence or otherwise of an author in the meaning of a literary work is a matter of choice, rather than an inviolable law. And despite this openness of interpretation of Morgan's poems, Mills also wants to leave us with a strong impression of Morgan's outlook on poetry; that he writes about science and contemporary life because they seem to him fit but largely ignored subjects for poetry; that he writes about what delights him in documentary detail, whilst still not telling us what to think; that he takes pleasure in language as material substance and plays with its possibilities. Mills leaves us with the image of a poet who raises important and interesting questions, and leaves us to answer them.

Mills' concern with what the reader brings to the reading of a poem is revisited in the next essay where Elizabeth Sandie writes about the poetry of **U.A. Fanthorpe**. She begins by addressing the task of the reader, who needs to know fairly quickly who is speaking and/or being addressed by the poem and what is expected of her or him. As a critic, she is aware that the many critical theories on offer will all have an 'angle' on Fanthorpe's writing, and she refers to such potential wherever relevant. But she also recognises the inevitable limitations of any theoretical approach, and warns us of the dangers: 'Whatever approaches we adopt, and as this book shows, there are lots of them, it is essential to keep the text alive.'

Sandie takes a view of Fanthorpe's work which is similar to my own view of Duffy when she says that her poems 'invite us to enter her social and geographical landscapes, stand beside her and see with her eyes.' As with the poetry of McMillan, Hattersley, Duffy and Clarke, we are told that Fanthorpe is concerned with marginal and marginalised people and lands. To this extent, Sandie points out, we could draw parallels between Fanthorpe's viewpoint and marxist or feminist theories. To the extent that Fanthorpe is concerned with how our understanding of texts shifts over time – and here we see the issue of reader-variation coming back in again – she is also a New Historicist, believing that the context of reception of a text will affect its meaning.

Some of Fanthorpe's achievement is measured by her use of form and language to symbolically represent her meaning. Sandie uses the poem

'Stanton Drew' to illustrate this point. It concerns a stone circle, but not Stonehenge, and she points out that the shape of the poem is visually monolithic and uses the pattern of syllables and caesuras to construct the alternation between longevity and life lived in the present. Sandie also points out some other linguistic features, such as deixis and register, thus to a degree using stylistic interpretation to back up her reading of Fanthorpe's poems. Ultimately, though, Sandie wants to assert that these poems have certain meanings, and she provides textual evidence of these meanings. Despite the recognition by both her and Fanthorpe that the reception of a poem cannot be anticipated, she argues strongly for particular interpretations when she feels that certain critics have 'got it wrong': 'Some readers have been known to be offended by the second stanza, but we have to hear the ironies here and think about the tone.'

The final essay in this collection concerns a remarkable book, *Birthday Letters*, published by **Ted Hughes** in the last year of his life and recording the events years earlier when he was married to Sylvia Plath. The subject matter, and thus the approach, are inevitably different again from the other chapters of this volume. Paul Mills takes the view that everyone, from teachers to creative writers, has something to learn from reading Hughes' last great work, and he substantiates this claim by exploring the book through an image of his own, that of the inverted cone. He claims that this image describes both the width of the experiences covered in *Birthday Letters* (the wide neck of the cone) and the claustrophobic restrictions of Hughes' relationship with Plath (the point of the cone). As the book progresses, he argues, Plath's own focus on her father, and death, becomes ever more insistent. However, Mills also explores the way in which Hughes is writing 'for the living, for survival', to demonstrate that exploring the imagination is not always and necessarily a self-destructive impulse, as it clearly was for Plath.

Mills hints at stylistic features of the writing in *Birthday Letters* that make me itch to follow them up. These include the use of pronouns, 'I' and 'you' as well as the sinister 'it' and the observation that most of the short sentences are broken still further by a line ending. However, his approach is generally much more literary, and includes the odd judgement, favourable or critical ('not Hughes at his best'), as well as indicating the ways in which the 'real life' stories on which these poems were based, are inextricably bound up with their interpretation. Mills claims that it was only through *not* being dragged down into the vortex of Plath's cone-shaped depression that Hughes managed to realise the powerful achievement of *Birthday Letters*, that he calls 'an unstoppable drama'.

It may be that many readers have not made it this far through the Introduction before dipping into the book. If you were my students, I'd recommend that you read it at the end anyway. What I have tried to demonstrate here is the way in which people from across the range of language and literary studies can respond to poems using their own analytical and critical techniques. What is striking to me is that very often we want to say the same kinds of things about the poems: how they show a shifting view of how life is categorised; how they are full of postmodern references to the fractured human identity that has been a theme throughout the twentieth century; how time place and person recur as themes in the poems of these peers.

What marks out the differences between these methods and approaches is the kinds of evidence or argument that are being put forward. They range from pure assertion, where the reader is expected to work out for themselves whether to agree or not to the relatively (despite Mackay) objective, where the evidence is marshalled and put up for scrutiny. The reader is still expected to weigh up the evidence, though the basis of the argument may be less implicit. In the middle, there are a range of approaches, many of them drawing on more than one theory or sub-discipline. They may draw in contextual evidence about how the poems were written, the life of the poet, the era of the composition, the tradition in which the poet is working or even the context in which the poem will be/is being read and by whom. There are also possibilities of combining the insights of a theory or theories with the methods of stylistics. Language can be assumed to be transparent, or it can be manipulated to reveal pattern not evident to the casual reader. And at one extreme, the text under consideration can be explored via other metaphors or images, conjured up by the commentator. With one or two exceptions, mostly when the approach is a writerly one, most of the approaches do not offer any kind of judgements about the poems' worth, though it seems unlikely to me that writers would choose to write about poetry they abhor, and there is thus often an implicit favourable judgement of the poems.

Lesley Jeffries

Lonely Meanings: Seamus Heaney's *The Spirit Level*

Ray Mackay

Introduction

In his review of Seamus Heaney's *The Spirit Level*, Nicholas Jenkins (1996) writes that it 'seeks out a more slippery and transitional state of being' and describes it as striving 'to be both buoyant and sombre'. In a similar vein, James Wood (1996) writes of 'Heaney's recent poetry [being] a poetry of release' and 'reality's ground [becoming] less important than the float of lyricism' while yet another critic claims that the poems in *The Spirit Level* 'aim for an unencumbered airiness of tone' (Wheatley, 1998).

In his book on Heaney's poetry, however, Neil Corcoran makes the following comment:

> In *The Spirit Level* the return from 'lightening' to another kind of self-burdening is apparent also in the language and forms of many of the poems ... *The Spirit Level* returns [Heaney] robustly to earth. (1998:192-193)

There is a very marked contrast here, with Wood and Wheatley seeing the poems in *The Spirit Level* as somehow giving an impression of lightness; Jenkins seeing them as 'both buoyant and sombre' and Corcoran identifying them as 'another kind of self-burdening'.

What is interesting about these critical observations, apart from the fact that they would each seem to be dealing with a different volume of poems, is that they are seldom supported by evidence from the poems themselves. It is true that reviews in such publications as *The Times Literary Supplement* or *The London Review of Books* tend not to go in for detailed literary criticism, favouring as they do the broad sweep; and it is the case that Corcoran adduces as evidence

Heaney's use of taboo words, Northern Ireland dialect words and expressions, and what he calls an 'offhandedness' (1998:193) in expressions like 'Or words to that effect', which appears in the poem 'The Flight Path'.

For students of literature, however, who might be searching for established critical markers to guide their own responses, such a diversity of responses might appear baffling. Is Corcoran correct in his evaluation? If he is, why didn't the other three critics see what he saw and come to the same conclusion? If, on the other hand, it is Corcoran who is wrong, what evidence is there to support the other three and what do we make of the evidence that Corcoran presents?

It is the purpose of this paper to explore and, if possible, explain, the discrepancies between these differing responses to Heaney's poems. (Such an exploration is fraught with difficulty because the only thing we can be reasonably sure of is that each of these four critics read the poems in *The Spirit Level*.) As a stylistician, that is to say, as someone interested in how responses are generated by language, it seems to me that a close examination of the words on these pages might go some way towards answering the questions posed above.

The paper is in four sections. Section 1 deals with the stylistic approach which I am adopting. Section 2 outlines a number of areas of investigation. These are, basically, the features of the poems which I believe might have given rise to the diversity of responses identified above. Section 3 examines one poem in detail, in the light of these features, and Section 4 is a Conclusion.

Subjective Stylistics

The essence of what 'subjective stylistics' means is captured by an image in a poem by W.S. Graham entitled 'The Constructed Space':

> ... of course we never know
> What we have said, what lonely meanings are read
> Into the spaces we made. And yet I say
> This silence here for in it I might hear you.
>
> I say this silence or, better, construct this space,
> So that somehow something may move across
> The caught habits of language to you and me.

We construct a space by engaging in the act of communication, Graham tells us, but we can 'never know' what our reader(s) or our listener(s) will make of what we've written or said. Their interpretations are 'lonely meanings' because we can 'never know' if our meaning has been conveyed. It is this basic scepticism that informs subjective stylistics. It is the same scepticism that caused Nietzsche to claim that all thinking was 'perspectival' and to declare that 'there are no facts, only interpretations' (Honderich, ed., 1995:622). At the heart of the communicative process is the individual act of interpretation and, because we are all individuals, with differing experiences of life and of language, there can be no certainty that any two individuals understand a piece of language in exactly the same way[1].

When I read and respond to a poem, I do not imagine that other readers will respond to the poem in the same way. Indeed, I expect them not to. So when I wrote in the Introduction about 'how responses are generated by language', I was not meaning to imply that language generates the same effects in all readers/listeners. Quite patently, in the light of the critical responses to Heaney's poems presented above, this would be an absurd claim. Similarly, if you accept this argument so far, you will also realise that the question as to whether Corcoran is correct in his evaluation is also absurd because, if there can be no guarantee of a single shared response, there is no way of judging 'correctness'. It is not the case that if the critics in question had paid sufficiently close attention to the language of the poems they would each have come to the same judgment as to their effect. (This point is picked up again in the Conclusion.)

There can be no set of objective criteria against which to measure these judgments because there can be nothing which is not interpreted by the individual. So what then is the role of stylistics? My position on this is as follows: I believe that when we read, we are often unaware of what it is about the language that causes us to respond in the way we do.

Discussing the role of syntax in poetry, Nowottny puts it like this:

> Of all the elements necessary to make an utterance meaningful, the most powerful is syntax, controlling as it does the order in

which impressions are received and conveying the mental
relations 'behind' sequences of words. And since we naturally
tend – except when checked by a difficulty – to take in without
effort the relations conveyed by syntax, its operation as a cause
of poetical pleasure is often the last we recognize, if indeed we
recognize it at all. (1962:9)

Nowottny's view is that a great deal may be going on in stretches
of poetic language that do not leap to the forefront of our attention.
(In a sense, this is the down-side of being native-speakers – we tend
to lose the awareness of what is actually happening as we process
language.) I think that she is right in this – and not only about syntax.

I believe that the study and practice of stylistic analysis has made
me (more) aware of (some of) the possible ways in which language
can generate effects in me as I engage in the process of reading. In
short, I am claiming to read differently from how Nowottny's reader
'naturally' tends to read. And I see it as my job to try to convince you
that what I see as significant in a text is what you should also view as
significant. I am, therefore, trying to change the way you read. There
are no 'facts' (i.e. nothing which stands outside of the interpretive
act) which I can use to persuade you that I am right. (There are, of
course, trivial facts, such as the fact that Heaney uses taboo words
such as 'camp-fucked' and 'cunt' in the poem 'Mycenae Lookout' –
as Corcoran points out. Corcoran's main point, however, is what
effect the use of such words has – and here he moves from fact to
opinion.) This means that I have to construct my argument well, if I
hope to convince you to accept it. The stylistic analysis you are about
to read is, then, a rhetorical construct – an exercise in persuasion[2].
Indeed, you should assume that this act of persuasion has already
commenced; by 'laying my cards' on the table, as it were, I am hoping
that this will generate in you a sense of trust in me.

As hinted at above, this section is concerned more with hypothesis
than with fact. It is a fact that literary critics have responded differently
to Seamus Heaney's *The Spirit Level*. The fundamental hypothesis
underlying this paper is that their differing responses might be
explicable if we assume that they were responding to different stimuli.
That is to say, for example, that when Corcoran read these poems he

attended to particular stretches of language and particular language features more than to others, which resulted in his gaining the impression of 'a kind of self-burdening' while Wheatley's attention was caught by different stretches of language and different language features from which he got the feeling that the very same poems seemed to aim for 'an unencumbered airiness of tone'. The question then becomes one of determining whether there is sufficient evidence in the text to support either of these two views.

Now it may be the case that this is not what happened. Instead, it may be the case that these two men attended to exactly the same stretches of language with exactly the same degree of attention but that they simply responded differently to them. This strikes me as being counter-intuitive. It seems unlikely that responding to the same stretches of language and language features could result in such widely-differing responses.

The assumption I have made, therefore, is that, if analysed from this perspective, the poems in *The Spirit Level* will reveal the presence of stretches of language and language features which suggest a sense of 'lightness', 'release', 'buoyancy', etc., and other stretches of language and language features which suggest the opposite – a sense of heaviness, of 'self-burdening'.

My task then becomes that of identifying the stylistic features which I believe might give rise to these responses and identifying whether such features are present in the poems themselves and to what extent.

Before moving on to the next section, it might be worthwhile for you to pause here and try to compile a list of such features yourself. If you wished to write a poem which gave the reader a sense of buoyancy, say, how would you set about it? And is it possible to compile a list of features that might do the opposite and generate a sense of heaviness?

Stylistic Features

I am now going to present a list of features that could be viewed as contributing to the responses noted above and discuss each one in detail, with reference to the poems. It is important to stress, however, that this list does not make any claim to objectivity. (After all, where could one go to check whether a particular feature of a poem actually did contribute to a sense of lightness, say?) I am not implying that the presence of these features leads automatically to a particular response being generated in readers. The limit of my claim is that I feel that the presence of these features has the potentiality for generating these responses in me as I read.

(i) lexis

This is perhaps the most obvious feature – it is certainly the one that Corcoran rests his case on. It seems to me that Corcoran is right in what he says: that the presence of swear words or dialect words would contribute to a sense of 'robustness', of 'heaviness' as opposed to 'lightness'. (I am not so sure that the use of expressions such as 'Or words to that effect', 'Or something like that' and 'And so on' serves the same function, as Corcoran claims (1998:193).)

But there are other interesting aspects of Heaney's use of lexis. Here are the first nine lines of 'To A Dutch Potter in Ireland':

> Then I entered a strongroom of vocabulary
> Where words like urns that had come through the fire
> Stood in their bone-dry alcoves next a kiln
>
> And came away changed, like the guard who'd seen
> The stone move in a diamond-blaze of air
> Or the gates of horn behind the gates of clay.
>
> The soils I knew ran dirty. River sand
> Was the one clean thing that stayed itself
> In that slabbery, clabbery, wintry, puddled ground.

It seems to me that there are two competing vocabularies at work here:

a) strongroom / kiln / stone / gates / clay / soil / dirty / sand
b) fire / bone-dry / diamond-blaze / air / clean

with set a) suggesting a sense of solidity and heaviness and set b) one of lightness. What seems to me to be characteristic of Heaney as a poet are the startling juxtapositions: 'a strongroom of vocabulary', 'words like urns', 'words … came away changed, like the guard..', 'the stone move in a diamond-blaze of air'. In each case, something very physical, very concrete, is set against something abstract, ephemeral.

Notice, too, that the dialect words 'slabbery, clabbery', which are, I take it, attempts at capturing the wet stickiness of the muddy ground, are juxtaposed to 'the one clean thing that stayed itself'. Again, one gets the feeling of heaviness being set against lightness.

The same effect can be seen, I think, in these lines from Part 1 of 'Mycenae Lookout':

> And then the ox would lurch against the gong
> And deaden it and I would feel my tongue
> Like the dropped gangplank of a cattle truck,
> Trampled and rattled, running piss and muck,
> All swimmy-trembly as the lick of fire,
> A victory beacon in an abattoir …

The ox itself is an embodiment of heaviness; to lurch is to make a heavy movement; a gong is a heavy object, as is the gangplank of a cattle truck: in six lines, weight is being piled upon weight. And, as in the previous example, Heaney offers a juxtaposition, this time with the startling neologism 'swimmy-trembly'. But here it works in the opposite direction, to convey a sense of lightness, which is continued with the phrases 'lick of fire' and 'victory beacon'. The final 'abattoir' seems to return us to the world of weight and heaviness. Startling too is the simile at the heart of this extract, that sensitive organ the tongue being compared to a 'dropped gangplank, running piss and muck'. The tightness of the vocabulary and imagery ('tongue' and 'lick', the ambiguity of 'rattled', the collocation of 'ox', 'cattle' and 'abattoir', the deadening of both sound and life) recalls the best of the Metaphysical poets, and the verse form (rhyming iambic pentameters) that could have come straight out of one of Shakespeare's plays, serve to remind us of the tradition from which Heaney's poetry comes. From the same poem, we can find many other examples of the same technique at work: 'My own mind was a bull-pen', 'The roof was like an ear-drum', 'ox-bowed/under his yoke of cloud'.

A further aspect of lexis also needs to be examined. It seems to me that if the vocabulary of a poem contained, say, a preponderance of abstract nouns as opposed to concrete nouns or a number of verbs relating to mental processes rather than physical actions, we would tend to get an impression of lightness. For example, here are all the nouns which occur in the first section of 'St Kevin and the Blackbird':

> St Kevin / blackbird / saint / arms / cell / palm / window / crossbeam / eggs / breast / head / claws / network / life / pity / hand / branch / sun / rain / weeks / young

and here are all the verbs:

> was / is kneeling / is / lands / lays / settles down / feels / is moved / must hold / are hatched / fledged / flown.

As can be seen, there are really only three abstract nouns in the list: 'network', 'life' and 'pity'; and only one verb ('is moved') relating to mental processes yet the impression I get on reading these lines is not one of heaviness but of lightness, which runs counter to my initial supposition. It seems to me that there are two ways to deal with this: I can either rethink my position on the effect of abstract vs concrete nouns and verbs relating to mental processes vs verbs relating to physical actions or try to retain my hypothesis by recontextualising the evidence. The first option doesn't appeal to me because I remain convinced that my initial supposition is correct. So I am left with the task of recontextualising the evidence, explaining the same phenomenon so that it makes sense, while not weakening my basic argument.

Notice how the poem begins:

> And then there was St Kevin and the blackbird.
> The saint is kneeling, arms stretched out …

The first line seems to suggest that this story – about the blackbird – is only one of many stories about St Kevin. (And, indeed, only one of the many mentions of saints in this collection.) The second line, however, with its shift to the present, takes us *into* the story itself. Heaney is attempting to present as vivid a picture as possible. With the beginning of the second section, however, everything changes:

And since the whole thing's imagined anyhow,
Imagine being Kevin.

This seems to me to be juxtaposing the real (the 'heavy') and the imaginary (the 'light') in much the same way as we have already seen, but this time on a larger scale. Rather than set lexis against lexis ('a strongroom of vocabulary', 'the stone move in a diamond-blaze of air'), here the poet is setting a very vivid (robust and down to earth) description within a larger, imaginary context, to which the first lines of each section alert us. On reflection, therefore, it should not be surprising that one gets a sense of lightness, of being detached ('the whole thing's imagined anyhow') while at the same time noting the down-to-earth quality of the vocabulary.

(ii) locatives

It seems to me that another way in which poetry might be tied down, as it were, weighted and burdened, is through the use of locatives – prepositional phrases which identify where the action is occurring. Conversely, poetry which didn't contain such phrases would seem likely to impart a rather distant, ungrounded, less encumbered quality.

'A Brigid's Girdle' is a poem of 20 lines and is full of locatives:

from a rustic table / under magnolias / on me / in the sunlit yard / plinkings from a dulcimer / migrating to the north / gathered in the earth / the first snowdrop in County Wicklow / lifted in a circle / going through the thing.

On the other hand, the second part of 'To A Dutch Potter in Ireland', 24 lines long, contains only four:

in a pearly clarity / in the near distance / five years on the rack/ the rye crop waves beside the ruins.

An obvious point to make in this connection is that where the nouns in these phrases are abstract, the effect is correspondingly diminished while, with concrete nouns, the effect is enhanced. Thus locatives such as 'from a rustic table', 'in the sunlit yard' and 'beside the ruins' serve to ground the poem while locatives such as 'in a pearly clarity' or 'in the near distance' contribute less to this effect. As with lexis, we can see that a sense of both lightness and heaviness is produced through Heaney's use of locatives.

(iii) imagery

Heaney's use of imagery in the poems in *The Spirit Level* is striking in
the way it juxtaposes just those notions of heaviness and lightness
which critics responded to and which are identified in the
Introduction. The very title *The Spirit Level*, of course, contributes
to this, with the notion of the builder's tool on the one hand and
some aspect of the human spirit on the other. What I propose to do
here is simply quote a number of instances of imagery from the poems
where an aspect of heaviness is juxtaposed to one of lightness and let
the mounting list speak for itself.

> And diminuendo runs through all its scales
> Like a gutter stopped trickling.
>   ('The Rain Stick')

In 'To A Dutch Potter in Ireland', clay is described as being 'Like
wet daylight/Or viscous satin'. In 'Damson', a trowel is described as

> … brightening itself by mucking in.
> It looked light but felt heavy as a weapon,
> Yet when he lifted it there was no strain,
> It was all point and skim and float and glisten.

In the poem 'Weighing In', we read how a 56lb weight –

> Gravity's black box, the immovable
> Stamp and squat and square-root of dead weight –

is balanced against a similar weight

> On a well-adjusted, freshly-greased weighbridge
> And everything trembled, flowed with give and take.

A sharping stone, in the poem of the same name, is described as 'a
baton of black light' while a blind musician in the poem 'At The
Wellhead' is described as being 'like a silver vein in heavy clay'. Most
startling of all, perhaps, is the line which occurs in 'The Swing',
which recalls the pleasure of children on a swing:

> We all learned one by one to go sky high.
> Then townlands vanished into aerodromes,

Hiroshima made light of human bones ...

The children are discovering the thrill of appearing to be weightless, of defying gravity. The poet then uses that very cunning 'then' to lead us into thinking that what we are going to read is the changed view of the world as seen by the children from the top of the swing's arc but instead, it has a larger, more historical reference. We discover how war changed the scenery both locally and globally and how the appalling triumph of the atomic bomb on Hiroshima was to render people literally weightless by first diminishing the importance (making light) of human bones (by dropping the bomb in the first place) and then vapourising these people, these bones, turning them into light in an atomic blast.

(iv) enjambement vs end-stopping

A fourth area of investigation relates to the form of the poems. It seems to me that if a poem has every line end-stopped, the effect on reading it will be to slow that reading down in a very predictable manner and so produce an effect of weightiness, of being encumbered. Here, for example, is Heaney describing a journeyman tailor:

> His lips tight back, a thread between his teeth,
> Keeping his counsel always, giving none,

> His eyelids steady as wrinkled horn or iron.
> Self-absenting, both migrant and ensconced ...
> ('At Banagher')

(Note also the way in which the eyelids are described – another light/heavy contrast. The phrase 'both migrant and ensconced' offers a contrast between a sense of absence and a sense of groundedness, which again reinforces the overall impression.)

By contrast, here is part of the poem 'Tollund', a significant location for Heaney as the site where the bodies of long-dead sacrificial victims were found in bog-land – the bodies and the events surrounding their deaths eventually becoming the subject of several of his most famous poems:

> It could have been a still out of the bright

> 'Townland of Peace', that poem of dream farms
> Outside all contention. The scarecrow's arms
> Stood open opposite the satellite
>
> Dish in the paddock, where a standing stone
> Had been resituated and landscaped …

The effect of the run-on lines (enjambement) is, I would argue, to speed up the reading and so produce a lighter feel to what is being read.

There are 35 poems in *The Spirit Level*, of which seven have an equal number of end-stopped to run-on lines, eighteen have fewer than half their lines end-stopped while ten have more. In total, out of 1268 lines of verse, almost 50% (607 lines) are end-stopped. I am aware as I write these figures that the enumeration of such data might appear a sad reflection on what stylistics involves. Even if you accept my arithmetic, these figures, by themselves, prove nothing. However, if you accept what I suggest concerning the effect of end-stopping/enjambement, then they become significant. Only by vesting them with the power to generate particular effects do they become so. In this light, given these figures, it is not surprising that people might respond differently to this collection of poems.

There are four other features which deserve mention: complex/simple sentences; monosyllabic/polysyllabic words; hypothetical/real statements and variations in sounds (longer, more open, voiceless sounds as opposed to shorter, more consonantal, voiced sounds). I mention these here because I began the planning of this paper by making a list of all the likely distinctions I could think of which might correlate with the effects of lightness or heaviness. After reading some of the poems through these lenses, as it were, I found that I could discern no obvious pattern. These represent, then, failed hypotheses as regards this stylistic analysis.

'Two Lorries'

In this section I propose to discuss one poem in detail, showing how the four features outlined above operate in the context of a complete poem. The poem I have chosen is 'Two Lorries'. It is worth making some brief points about the poem first. It is a sestina; that is to say, it contains six verses of six lines each, followed by a three line coda. The end word of each line in verse one reappears as an end word of each line of all five other verses in a shifting pattern. The last three lines contain all these end words. This formal patterning is important because the way in which the poet sometimes repeats, sometimes varies, these end words is, I feel, significant.

Two Lorries
It's raining on black coal and warm wet ashes.
There are tyre-marks in the yard, Agnew's old lorry
Has all its cribs down and Agnew the coalman
With his Belfast accent's sweet-talking my mother.
Would she ever go to a film in Magherafelt?
But it's raining and he still has half the load

To deliver farther on. This time the lode
Our coal came from was silk-white, so the ashes
Will be the silkiest white. The Magherafelt
(Via Toomebridge) bus goes by. The half-stripped lorry
With its emptied, folded coal-bags moves my mother:
The tasty ways of a leather-aproned coalman!

And films no less! The conceit of a coalman …
She goes back in and gets out the black lead
And emery paper, this nineteen-forties mother,
All business round her stove, half-wiping ashes
With a backhand from her cheek as the bolted lorry
Gets revved up and turned and heads for Magherafelt

And the last delivery. Oh, Magherafelt!
Oh, dream of red plush and a city coalman
As time fastforwards and a different lorry
Groans into shot, up Broad Street, with a payload
That will blow the bus station to dust and ashes …
After that happened, I'd a vision of my mother,

A revenant on the bench where I would meet her
In that cold-floored waiting-room in Magherafelt,
Her shopping bags full up with shovelled ashes.
Death walks out past her like a dust-faced coalman
Refolding body-bags, plying his load
Empty upon empty, in a flurry

> Of motes and engine-revs, but which lorry
> Was it now? Young Agnew's or that other,
> Heavier, deadlier one, set to explode
> In a time beyond her time in Magherafelt ...
> So tally bags and sweet-talk darkness, coalman.
> Listen to the rain spit in new ashes
>
> As you heft a load of dust that was Magherafelt,
> Then reappear from your lorry as my mother's
> Dreamboat coalman filmed in silk-white ashes.

(i) lexis

It seems to me that, from the point of view of lexis, this poem divides into two. The profusion of concrete nouns in the first three stanzas serve to ground the poem in a vividly described reality: lorries, black coal, wet ashes, tyre-marks, yard, cribs, coalman, mother, load – to select from the first stanza only. The fourth stanza ushers in a more complex lexical patterning, with the on-going vivid description (bus station, dust, ashes, bench, shopping bags, etc.) being set against a more unreal, detached imagining – dream, vision, revenant, Death, time, darkness. This culminates in the last two lines with the terrorist disguised as a coalman reappearing as his mother's 'dreamboat coalman', but 'filmed' in the 'silk-white ashes' of his childhood memories and the 'silk-white ashes' caused by the bombing. Here there is a fusion of effects. Clearly, there is a sense of 'heaviness', of rootedness, generated by the vividness with which Heaney captures details of his childhood. There is, likewise, a sense of heaviness generated by the subject matter itself – the transportation and delivery of coal on the one hand and, on the other, terrorists weighing down a 'heavier, deadlier' coal lorry with explosives and using it as a weapon.

At the same time, there is a sense of detachment, of floating free from this reality. This is generated first in a positive manner by the references to films and the sense of Hollywood romance (sweet-talking my mother, dream of red plush, dreamboat coalman) and also more darkly by the poet's 'vision' of his mother in Magherafelt on the day of the bombing as a ghost ('revenant'), with Death walking past her and the terrorist coalman sweet-talking not his mother but 'darkness'.

The poet's use of verbs, however, seems to work against the pattern established by the nouns in that he uses a comparatively large number of verbs relating to physical action in the 'vision' section of the poem 'would meet', 'walked out', 'refolding', 'plying') and comparatively fewer in the first part.

I think we can see ample evidence here of how two contrary impressions are being generated almost simultaneously, evidence which, in turn, explains the responses of the critics referred to in the Introduction.

Because of the very formal structuring of this poem, it is worth looking in detail at what Heaney does with the six end-words, perhaps the main defining characteristic of the sestina form. The words 'coalman', 'Magherafelt' and 'ashes' remain the same throughout the six stanzas and the 3-line coda but the other three words – 'mother', 'lorry' and 'load' – undergo transformation, much as they did in real life. The coal 'lorry' and its innocent victims are blasted into a 'flurry' while the central point of the poem – the 'load' which the coal lorry carried – is transformed from the second stanza, as though to prepare us for what is to come: load > lode > lead > payload > load > explode > load. Most charged of all is the change from 'mother' to 'meet her'. Meeting his mother again in a vision allows the poet the historical perspective from which to contrast the innocence of the 'nineteen-forties' and the modern reality of life in a city ravaged by acts of terrorist violence.

(ii) locatives

As we might now have learned to expect, Heaney uses these frequently throughout his poem, but in a very particular manner. From the first four stanzas of the poem, we find:

> on black coal / in the yard / in Magherafelt / round her stove /
> from her cheek / for Magherafelt / into shot / up Broad Street

culminating in the very specific locative at the beginning of stanza five – 'in that cold-floored waiting-room in Magherafelt'.

After Death walks past his mother 'in a flurry/Of motes and engine revs', everything becomes much less specific, an impression strengthened by the question: '... but which lorry/Was it now?' until we move to 'a time beyond her time in Magherafelt ... ' and we return again to the rain. But this time it's not 'raining on black coal and warm wet ashes' but spitting 'in new ashes'.

(iii) imagery

Apart from the cinematic 'time fastforwards' and the lorry 'groan[ing] into shot' in stanza four and the 'dreamboat coalman' in the last line, Heaney minimises his use of imagery in this poem. In stanza five, he sees his mother's ghost and Death walking past her 'like a dust-faced coalman', the only simile in the poem. I think it is possible to explain this if we consider that imagery brings another element into our thinking, either as a comparison or as another way of seeing the thing itself. This doubleness is already accomplished in 'Two Lorries' in a number of ways: the historic fact of the two coal lorries (and the two coalmen), one bringing warmth, contact, a hint of romance, the other bringing death and destruction; the way in which Heaney recaptures his mother in life, as it were, and then presents her again as a ghost; the way in which the everyday, working-class life of a begrimed coalman and a 'nineteen-forties mother' cleaning her stove with 'black lead' is transformed into a 'dream of red plush' and a 'dreamboat coalman'; and it is this doubleness which charges with extra meaning words and expressions like 'go to a film', 'ashes', 'the last delivery', and so on.

(iv) enjambement

In terms of enjambement vs end-stopping, this poem has almost half (17 out of 39) of its lines end-stopped. Interestingly, three of these lines don't end with a full stop or comma, etc., but simply tail away:

(i)   The conceit of a coalman ...
(ii) That will blow the bus station to dust and ashes ...
(iii) In a time beyond her time in Magherafelt ...

As we read the poem, these generate a sense of unfinished business, as though matters were being left in suspension. In the first example, the word 'conceit' contains multiple meanings which we only become aware of in the context of the whole poem: the coalman is conceited to think that he can invite a married woman to go to a film with him; more importantly, there is a metaphysical conceit buried in the request to 'go to a film in Magherafelt' because another 'coalman', at a much later date, was conceited enough to believe that he was right to drive a coal lorry full of explosives into the town and destroy people such that they became 'a film' of ashes. The second example allows the poet to move out of historical time because it is followed immediately with the line 'After that happened, I'd a vision of my mother' while the third example takes us back from that 'time beyond her time'.

The effect of these is to loosen reality's grip on what is being described, to provide a sense of detachment, of lightness.

Conclusion

The motivating force behind this paper was the need to explain a diversity of critical responses to Seamus Heaney's *The Spirit Level* and I hope that, to some extent at least, I have achieved that goal.

I began by arguing that a close examination of the language of the poems might shed some light on the issue and this I take to be one of the main purposes of stylistics – its use as an explanatory tool. The approach taken, subjective stylistics, eschewed any claim to objectivity. Indeed, I argued that, where language is concerned, objectivity is simply not possible because of the radically indeterminate nature of the act of interpretation. In most everyday circumstances, the communicational context is constrained sufficiently through what W.S.Graham calls 'the caught habits of language' to allow us to proceed as though there were no problem – and often, indeed, no problem arises. But a work of literature is not constructed so as to communicate in that way and the multiplicity of ways in which we, the readers, can differ in what we take to the interpretive act, must affect what we take from that interaction.

As there can therefore be no way, in my opinion, of adjudicating on the absolute rightness or wrongness of a response to a work of literature, judgments as to the 'rightness' of a response become, in fact, judgments as to the power of the arguments used to support a particular response. In short, the literary response supported by the most persuasive argument becomes the 'right' response until an even more persuasive argument comes along. There is always a right response – but it isn't always the same one[3]. What this paper has found is that there appears to be equally persuasive evidence to support the various differing responses with which we began. There are two characteristics of a subjective stylistic analysis which you may have noticed. The first is the frequent uses of subjective markers like 'I think…', 'I feel…', 'I believe…' and the second is that your attention was drawn to the fact that an attempt was being made to persuade you. Furthermore, in one instance, I drew attention to the fact that part of my initial supposition had failed and, in a second, that I had to make another argumentative move to account for an apparent anomaly. This, I believe, is how stylistics should be practised.

Finally, I should say that even although you may have accepted my argument regarding differing responses to the poems in *The Spirit Level*, the argument does not stop here. How general is my argument with respect first to Heaney's other poetry and, secondly, to poetry in general? Is it the case that impressions of lightness or heaviness (and I should add here that I am happier using 'lightness' than I am using 'heaviness', which seems to me a more confusing concept) are only generated by the four features I have identified? Are there other language features that I have not thought of which could generate similar responses? Do the features I thought of but subsequently rejected have any part to play in the broader picture? Is it the case that where the four features mentioned occur in other poems there is always a sense of lightness/heaviness? Do these features (with the exception of enjambement/end-stopping) generate the same types of response in prose? How typical were the responses of the four critics quoted anyway?

As far as I am concerned, however, the big picture is not the practice of stylistics as an end itself but more as a means of trying to understand responses to language; to understand, for example, why these, the last lines from the poem 'Postscript', and the last in *The Spirit Level*, are so moving and evocative:

You are neither here nor there,
A hurry through which known and strange things pass
As big soft buffetings come at the car sideways
And catch the heart off guard and blow it open.

NOTES

[1]This point is elaborated in Mackay (1996). I should add that this position, and its consequences if adopted by stylisticians, has been the subject of some debate. See Short, et al (1998), Mackay (1999) and Short & van Peer (1999) for details.

[2] I would argue, of course, that all stylistic analyses are rhetorical constructs but that the stylisticians who espouse 'objective' stylistics have forgotten that their bags of tricks (the use of models, the use of statistical analysis, etc.) are there to persuade us of the rightness of their arguments. Unless you 'come out' as regards rhetoric, it is always the case that it's the other person's problem; you only want 'the plain, unvarnished truth' as opposed to the varnished variety.

[3] This point is made (very frequently!) by Stanley Fish (1989).

BIBLIOGRAPHY

Corcoran, N. (1998) *The Poetry of Seamus Heaney,* Faber & Faber

Fish, S. (1989) *Doing What Comes Naturally,* Clarendon Press, Oxford.

Heaney, S. (1996) *The Spirit Level* Faber & Faber

Honderich, T. (ed) (1995) *The Oxford Companion to Philosophy* Oxford University Press

Jenkins, N. (1996) 'Walking on air – travel and release in Seamus Heaney' *The Times Literary Supplement* July 5, 1996.

Mackay, R. (1996) 'Mything the Point: A Critique of Objective Stylistics' *Language and Communication* 16 (1): 81-93.

Mackay, R. (1999) 'There Goes The Other Foot – A Reply to Short et al' *Language and Literature* 8 (1): 59-66.

Nowottny, W. (1962) *The Language Poets Use* The Athlone Press, London.

Short, M., et al (1998) 'Stylistics, criticism and mythrepresentation again: squaring the circle with Ray Mackay's subjective solution for all problems' *Language and Literature* 7 (1): 39-50.

Short, M. & W. van Peer (1999) 'A Reply To Mackay' *Language and Literature* 8 (3): 269-275.

Wheatley, (1998) 'Heelmark in poetry's landscape' *Times Higher Education Supplement*, November 20, 1998.

Wood, J. (1996) 'Scruples' *London Review of Books,* Vol 18 (12).

Acknowledgement: I am grateful to my colleague, David Carver, for reading this paper and discussing it with me.

Coining Phrases: Cliché and Creativity in the Poetry of Tony Harrison

Geoff Hall

Introduction

A growing body of research has documented the centrality and pervasiveness of fixed expressions, including clichés, in everyday spoken interaction. Latterly, corpus-based research and pragmatics have deepened our knowledge of the constituents, forms and uses of fixed expressions. Lakoff and Johnson (1980) have drawn attention to the 'clichés we live by' in social life, which organise our established realities, just as social and cultural historians have stressed the cohesive and strategic roles played by fixed expressions in the negotiation and constitution of social and cultural identities.

Writers on literary discourse, by contrast, have traditionally proclaimed a post-Romantic ideology of creativity, originality and spontaneity of expression, for which the clichéd expression is anathema. This ideology still dominates evaluations of written production through writing guides and schoolteachers' pronouncements to professors of literature. In this perspective, clichés are mechanical, dead, and lack individuality or expressiveness. Ironically, even where such creative uses of language can be found, Lakoff and Turner (1989) have documented the extent to which such literary creativity depends upon less salient founding metaphorical cognitive structures.

'Make it new' itself became the established cliché of modernism in particular. Thus, while clichés are surprisingly frequent in canonical modernist writings like Eliot's 'The Waste Land', or in Larkin's mostly pained and distanced poetic explorations of everyday life, the attitude is generally firmly patronising and the occurrence of clichés, often typographically italicised, while a gesture to Bakhtinian 'novelisation', serves in the main to underline the unbridgeable gulfs between poet and people, us and them, the programme of knowing winks and nudges Leavisian literary studies was instituted to promote. The ideas and beliefs of ordinary people in their everyday life are held up for the inspection of poetry reading élites and generally found wanting. Poetry after Eliot is 'a raid on the inarticulate' ('Four Quartets'), cliché suitable generally only for comic effects (see also Carter 1987: 199 on Auden; Moon 1998).

Tony Harrison's declared poetic programme is to bridge this gap, to render poetry less esoteric and more accessible, precisely to contest the élitism of modernist and wider modern literary practices. He writes in part to uphold the validity of the everyday working class Northern English culture into which he was born, while not denying the value of his own education in literature and the classics, despite the attitudes and ideologies through which it is constructed. Not coincidentally, the most frequent criticism made of Tony Harrison's poetry is of bad taste, 'mawkishness', a too ready accessibility to ordinary readers at the expense of reducing all his subjects (including Bosnia, the Gulf War, classic drama) to the known and familiar and everyday. Familiarity breeds contempt is the (of course unwritten!) cliché informing the response of these critics.

In this chapter I propose to demonstrate Harrison's regular even insistent use of cliché as a deliberately provocative gesture of solidarity with the culture of his background, or, more than a gesture, an attempt at shared communication across cultural divides which insists on the value of popular perceptions and ways of living. Beyond this, I wish to ask how far Harrison's homely language has limited the reach and value of his poetry as his detractors claim. I will present Harrison's poetry from a Bakhtinian perspective as dialogical and heteroglossic, from the early and generally highly regarded 'School for Eloquence' sonnets to his more recent writings, whose value is more contested, including the 'Prometheus' film released in 1999, where reviewers objected with derision or well-bred disgust to the jarring rhymed question:

> How can Olympus stay intact
> If poetry comes to Pontefract?

The wider issues raised by this study concern the linguistic nature of creative writing and the question of literary value, as well as a possible shift in literary forms in developments since the dominance of modernism in English poetic writing in the earlier part of the twentieth century.

Cliché

Cliché is a cultural evaluation of language use rather than an objectively identifiable linguistic category, 'convenient reach-me-downs' that can be 'taken off the peg' and used 'mechanically', 'as the fittest way of saying what needs to be said' (Fowler 1983: 91; see also 'hackneyed phrases' entry; also Zijderveld 1979: 6). Not all idioms or fixed collocations are invariably described as cliché , though most can be so described by a sufficiently hostile reader or overhearer. Above all, clichés are supposed to represent popular ('of the people') sentimentalisms of a kind a higher sensibility, or at least higher education, trains the more sophisticated language user to see the inadequacy of. The lack of creativity in such language use, we are told, indexes a more fundamental lack of original thought or understanding. A central irony (Ricks 1993) is that the supposedly 'dead' or dying phrases are most commonly spoken, and therefore perhaps, it could be argued, in a sense most alive. We will return to this paradox. At least, for the moment, it should be noted that while clichés can seem frustratingly vague, inadequate and impersonal, at times of pronounced personal emotional feelings (notably, on occasions of death), somehow no other form of words sounds as appropriate, much as the afflicted will themselves turn for solace to poetry or song, even though these are not their 'own' words. Other social occasions linked to use of cliché are the rituals surrounding births, marriages, or religious ceremonies. Why do we often hesitate so long over exactly which tacky birthday card to buy for someone who truly matters to us? Clichés, in short, can be invested with a great deal of affect.

Symptomatically, from Partridge's *Dictionary of Clichés* (1940) to the Bloomsbury *Dictionary of Clichés* (1996), it is agreed that clichés are not easy to define, but that you (the educated reader) should know one when you see one. Another 'distinction' (Bourdieu 1979/ 1984) between 'them' and 'us'. Etymologically, such reference works inform us, the 'cliché' is an image taken from the era when western industrial methods began to facilitate mass printing at ever cheaper rates and greater speeds, and so, potentially, literacy of the masses. A 'cliché', or more transparently still, a 'stereotype', referred originally to a mould for steam presses which would be used to reprint exactly the same words many times without breaking down. The word 'cliché' appears in French in 1809 to describe this technological breakthrough, but soon crosses the channel to appear in nineteenth century reviews (there was now a need for guardians of public taste, the reviewers) to attack metaphorically the prefabricated language observed in novels condemned as pot boilers for an unsophisticated audience of English readers (Lynch 1998).

It is important then to note that a notion of clichéd writing develops historically in tandem with, if not *as part of the constitution of,* a distinction between 'good' and 'hackneyed' writing, above all in opposition to the new valorised category of 'Literature'. This distinction would enable the educated to recognise themselves and to distinguish their own sensibilities from those of the 'illiterate' crowd. Eighteenth century 'decorum' evolved into the modern sociolinguist's 'appropriacy': one just doesn't write such things. By the nineteenth century, with the development of an economic system of publishing based on authors, copyright and the like, inverted commas began to be used to signal ownership or attribution of language, or to distance the author from words of others, where in the seventeenth century inverted commas were used for dicta, proverbs, the authorless/ collectively-authored linguistic wisdom known to be common property of the whole society (Lynch 1998). Similarly, Obelkevich (1987) notes that with the Romantic onslaught on 'received ideas', a shift took place from positive to negative connotations of words like 'sententious' or 'commonplace'.

In sum, the modern idea of a cliché is particularly bound up with the historical move from an oral-traditional to a modern literate culture, mediated in particular by the Romantic response to the industrial revolution. In traditional societies (Ong 1967, Coulmas

1981), formulaic utterances, proverbs and fixed expressions are typically valued as shared collective and traditional wisdom. The value of coins, as Benjamin points out in 'The Work of Art in the Age of Mechanical Production' (1936/1973), lies precisely in their ability to be reproduced faithfully and in quantity. In the era of advanced capitalism, however, to 'coin a phrase' became a devalued form of cultural action unless the coin was new-minted. Thus Orwell, in his celebrated 'Politics and the English Language' essay, objects to cliché (among others), because: 'A speaker who uses that kind of language has gone some distance towards turning himself into a machine' (152). While the psycholinguist and conversational analyst alike would agree that a large component of speech or writing is the prefabricated 'automatically' processed phrase, there was nothing new about this in the twentieth century. What was new, with the recent experiences of fascism in Europe, was the increasing distrust of the language of others, and the Romantic preference, in written expression especially, for the organic over the mechanical, Literature over literature, even as language and literature became ever more commodified and privatised.

Literature, then, emerged as a category and defined itself against popular literature, the 'clichés' of popular journalism, 'penny dreadfuls' and the residual oral tradition of working class comedians and the urban music hall. (Altick 1976). It was left to the generation of Hoggart (1957), Raymond Williams and Tony Harrison (see the joint dedication of 'Them and Us' to comedian Leon Cortez[1] and Richard Hoggart), and later the Birmingham Centre for Contemporary Cultural Studies and others, to reclaim this devalued popular cultural tradition with its threatening (to middle class investigators) catch phrases, 'antilanguages' (Halliday 1978), solidarities and 'knowingness' (Bailey 1994). Cultural élites from Plato to the present day have distrusted poetry and proverbial sayings which mean more than they seem to say. At the same time, silence or inarticulacy (not the same thing obviously) are feared or resented by those whose careers and identities are built upon personal linguistic facility and creativity, as opposed to the false fluency clichés seem to offer. The dominant linguistic perspectives on cliché have been those of Chomsky, for whose confessedly idealised model human language is creative or it is nothing, and of psycholinguistics, in many ways Chomsky's child, which recognises cliché as a necessary if regrettable performance strategy to enable cognitive processing to take place. The perspective in this essay is more pragmatic and sociolinguistic, as we ask who uses clichés, at what points in the creation of text, and for what social purposes. I also propose that whereas, in everyday use of cliché, function typically supersedes meaning (compare Stubbs 1983), in Harrison's poetry, because it *is* poetry (Jakobson 1960), the meaning as well as the function of cliché are explored.

Harrison

Harrison is always keen to represent himself as 'the man who came to read the metre' (Hebert 1985), an everyday, workman-like activity, though signalling too (here through the metre/ meter pun) the particular awareness of language the poet needs to bring to his craft.

For many readers and critics, Harrison's most sustained achievement to date remains the ongoing autobiographical sonnet sequence, 'The School for Eloquence', itself a characteristically motivated reference to E.P. Thompson's classic *The Making of the English Working Class* (1963), published by another member of the 'new left' generation of grammar school scholarship boys with working class backgrounds or connections (Extra-Mural Lecturer for Leeds University), including Raymond Williams (*Culture and Society 1780-1950,* 1958) and, also from Leeds, Richard Hoggart (*The Uses of Literacy,* 1957). The sequence is dedicated to Harrison's father and the poet has gone on record as believing that the value of these sonnets lies in his gradually developing the ability to write in a language that would not exclude those of his working class background he would like to believe he writes for. One way in which this greater accessibility and more ordinary tone of language is achieved – the focus of this chapter – is through the use of cliché and intertextual ventriloquising of the personal and cultural history clichés speak from.

Even the most casual reader will have noticed the regular occurrence of idioms in Harrison's work (to avoid evaluating such language as cliché), and as I mentioned earlier, this is one of the easiest targets for parodists. 'Your bed's got two wrong sides' (133), Cagney movies are 'up both our streets' (143). In the first instance these utterances are attributable in context to individual speakers (Harrison's father, Harrison, respectively). But behind these individuals lies the shared culture which recognises and values these shared ways of viewing and talking about the world.

More significant still, my relatively open cataloguing of clichés in the sonnets quickly revealed significant formal patterning in the incidence and apparent function of these idioms. Appreciation of this point requires some background information on the form of the sonnets. 'Sonnets', indeed, may be something of a misnomer for the purist who looks for self-sufficient twelve line verbal icons. Harrison's sonnets in this sequence are by contrast Meredithian, that is, part of an ongoing narrative sequence, and most noticeably different from the classical model in having sixteen lines. Harrison has reported in interview that twelve lines were 'not enough' for him to include the voices of his mother and father, but above all to maintain the dominant narrative impetus of the sequence as a whole. Typically, then, the Harrison sonnet (at least the more obviously personal ones) takes the form of four quatrains, with an alternating ABAB, CDCD, etc. rhyme scheme, with, crudely, a situation sketched, some telling event or incident at the centre, and some kind of 'moral' or 'Evaluation' in Labov's terms, pointing up the meaning of the remembered incident for the poet in the present. The salient fact is that most of the clichés I identified (that is idioms particularly likely to provoke charges of bad taste, lack of original thought and the rest) occur at three pivotal positions: first, as title ('The Queen's English', 'Grey Matter', 'An Old Score', 'The Morning After') or in the first line: ('Your bed's got two wrong sides' (133), 'up both our streets' (143). Second, as concluding lines, often as concluding words: 'I can't put you down' (141), 'midnight oil' (145), 'The penny dropped in time. Wish you were here.' (146). These occurrences at the beginning or end of a poem arguably serve a kind of synoptic or framing function for the narrative which precedes or follows. I will return to this point in the light of findings from poetics and conversational analysis.

The third point in the sonnets at which I identify many clichés is at line thirteen or fourteen, (or twelve: 'just popped out to get the tea', 134), i.e. at the transition to or at the opening of the final quatrain in which the reader looks for some kind of conclusion or resolution to emerge: 'He never begged. For nowt! (149), 'I'm opening my trap' (149), 'good reads' (141). This third place of occurrence, like the first two, presents the clichés affectionately, even authoritatively. It is worth noting that when, more rarely, clichés are found in non-topic transitional positions ('the family circle', 147, 'my daily bread', 155), they seem to be intended ironically, and are arguably more middle class or conventional in origin or reference (less marked as 'Northern working class').

Harrison's use of clichés, then, in the 'School for Eloquence' series, is evidently not casual or careless, however tasteless it might seem to some as a poetic strategy. It is rather a demonstrably integral part of the structural design of a highly structured poetic form. I wish to argue for the effectiveness of these clichés used to frame structural movements and used in particular to conclude some of the most successful of the sonnets. It is here particularly relevant to invoke the poetics and pragmatics of closure, before turning to one poem in particular, 'Illuminations I', to illustrate in more detail the workings of cliché in a powerful sonnet, including, to my judgement, a devastating cliché closure.

Barbara Herrnstein Smith, in *Poetic Closure* (1968), a stimulating study which originated in the study of conclusions of English Renaissance sonnets, investigates the 'sense of finality, stability and integrity', even of 'truth' effected by successful closure of a poem. Poetic closure, she suggests, is a matter of both structure and form (rhyme, fixed number of lines, slowing of metre, hyperbole/ absence of modalisation, or other phonological or linguistic patterning which leads the reader to expect closure at the appropriate point), and of theme or content (poems will often conclude with references to death. or lexical items like 'finished', 'end', 'rest', 'peace', 'no more'). All such devices will work to convince the reader that the close of a poem (if successful) is in some sense a 'last word'. Significantly, Keats' 'Ode on a Grecian Urn' is instanced as one of the most consummate closures in English poetry, instancing many of the typical features and so poetically convincing if not (as the history of criticism will bear witness) entirely lucid from a logical point of view:

> 'Beauty is truth, truth beauty,' – that is all
> Ye know on earth, and all ye need to know. (195)

Harrison refers wryly to a 'well wrought urn' at line ten of 'Bringing Up' as he remembers his parents' suspicion of his 'clever' (and obscene) youthful poetry. His admiration for Keats is particularly evident in the poem 'A Kumquat for John Keats' (1981), which he likes to read in public, and in which he balances an evident Romantic relish for language with a more pedestrian autobiographical narrative line.

Evidence of poetic closure, as more widely understood in the classic study of the topic, is clearly observable in Harrison's reflections on his relations with his deceased parents. Contributing to the sense of closure of his more successful poems is the determinate length of a fixed sonnet form, patterning, rhyme schemes, absence of modalisation/ use of declarative and generic sentences and the rest. Similarly, the topics are often of completed episodes, never to be revisited, including funerals, last visits, deaths and cemeteries. What Smith's study does not lead us to expect, however, is the use of cliché-as-clincher which is so typical of Harrison's sonnets, 'Punchline' in his own word (p150). Here it is more fruitful to turn to the study of the everyday language Harrison wishes his poetry, in some ways, (notably accessibility) to approximate to.

Pragmatics and more recently corpus lexicology have much to offer the student of cliché, including empirical evidence for the use of cliché as closure of topic or of an entire conversation. Thus Stubbs (1983), in a study of narrative in casual conversations, observes: 'One way to signal the end of a story in casual conversation is to use a cliché-cum-proverb with little informational content', instancing from his own data conversations closing with utterances such as '"Still, that's life; Well, that's the way it goes; But something may turn up – you never know; Still, we may as well hope for the best... [and] ... it makes you think."' (24). Stubbs notes the lack of 'new propositional content' in such instances, confirming the suspicion that participants in such conversations are right to take these clichés as 'markers of the end of the story, and not as resources for further talk.' (24)

'Resources for further talk', in fact, sounds like an intertextual reference to conversational analysis, and it is this school of pragmatics research which offers a richer interpretation of the reasons for incidence of clichés. Thus, for example, in the classic Schegloff and Sacks essay 'Opening up Closings' (1973), the authors note the common use of 'a proverbial or aphoristic formulation of conventional wisdom which can be heard as the 'moral' or 'lesson' of the topic being thereby closed' (306), for example: '"Yeah well, things uh always work out for the best"', to which Theresa's interlocutor, Dorrinne replies: '"Oh certainly. Alright."' (307). There is an authoritative resonance to such clichés, yet which valuably combines with a convenient vagueness of meaning. In such data clichés typically seem to offer a linguistic formulation of a situation both parties can be content with, when neither wish to pursue potential differences any further.

It is precisely this aspect that is pursued in Drew and Holt's paper on the use of cliché in the negotiation of complaints, a paper which has much enriched my reading of the Harrison instances, though such powerful resonances can never have been intended by the authors. Thus, they note, clichés are a means of 'casting private troubles or anxieties into the public domain', especially in 'inauspicious environments', where interlocutors may not be fully sympathetic, or at least cannot fully share the aggrieved's perspective. (398) Without trivialising Harrison's grief over the death of his parents in any way, I note, for example, Emma, in Drew and Holt's data, who lists a number of failings of service in a hotel she visited with her husband and son, in much the way Harrison will tell a narrative of his earlier life, concluding: '"I mean that's how bad the service was. It's gone to pot.' (401). Indeed, I would say that my reading of Harrison lent unsuspected depth, even pathos, to others of Drew and Holt's complainants 'banging [their] heads against a brick wall', or 'throw[n] off the deep end' (403), or 'between the devil and the deep blue sea' (411), among others. These are real people, often discussing very serious personal predicaments, including the breakdown of a marriage or debt problems, as well as problems with hotels and restaurants, who turn instinctively to metaphor and cliché in expressing their crises and asking for sympathy from fellow human beings. Drew and Holt in fact suggest that these metaphorical qualities are a crucial element in explaining why such language is reached for at such moments: 'This may give such expressions a special robustness: since they are not to be taken literally, they may have a certain resistance to being tested or challenged on the empirical facts of the matter.' (406) Thus closure can be achieved, with sympathy, at least on the surface, evoked: it is difficult to disagree with a cliché by its very nature. Similarly, Moon (1998), observes from her study of fixed expressions in naturally occurring corpus data, that idioms are used in persuading interlocutors to share an orientation to a problem or situation (245), or, quoting Obelkevich (1987, quoted 258): '"people use proverbs to tell others what to do in a given situation or what attitude to take towards it."'

But perhaps poetry should be different, not simply reproducing the clichés of everyday stresses and strains as what I have called the Romantic ideology of Literature would have us believe? That the use of cliché in poetry can be very successful is a key tenet of this essay, and I will now offer a more extended example than hitherto from a Harrison sonnet in support of this proposition:

Illuminations

I

The two machines on Blackpool's Central Pier,
The Long Drop and *The Haunted House* gave me
my thrills the holiday that post-war year
but my father watched me spend impatiently:

Another tanner's worth, but then no more!

But I sneaked back the moment that you napped.
50 weeks of ovens, and 6 years of war
made you want sleep and ozone, and you snapped:

Bugger the machines! Breathe God's fresh air!

I sulked all week, and wouldn't hold your hand.
I'd never heard you mention God, or swear,
and it took me until now to understand.

> I see now all the piled old pence turned green,
> enough to hang the murderer all year
> and stare at millions of ghosts in the machine –
>
> The penny dropped in time! Wish you were here!

'Illuminations I' is in many ways a key representative of the phenomenon and features I have discussed, valued by admirers and likely to be pilloried by critics. The poem is a narrative of an early family holiday in the wake of the second world war, a visit, as the punning title intimates, to Blackpool. The first quatrain sets the scene in a third person mode. Typically the second quatrain moves to a new mode with the dramatised voice of the (now deceased) father speaking (in 'ordinary', 'everyday' language) and framing the second quatrain's development of the narrative, including the transition to the third quatrain, which reports the young Harrison's response to his father's exasperation. The conclusion to the third quatrain promises 'understanding' of this episode, as formal requirements would lead us to expect. We move to a vatic or bardic present tense perception, as much metaphorical as literal, 'I see now'. 'Millions of ghosts in the machine' characteristically combines intertextually a childish hyperbolic register with allusions to Koestler or perhaps Pascal; certainly the reference is to the uncertainties of life after death and a spiritual realm, beyond the literal 'work of art in the age of mechanical reproduction'. I find the concluding line, typographically and symbolically isolated, conclusively moving where others will no doubt hear only pathetic sentimentality: 'The penny dropped in time! Wish you were here!' Again a childish expression is used to metaphorically refer to understanding in a pun derived from the slot machine situation. But the real achievement for this closure, I would argue, is the startling renovation of one of the most worn our phrases in the language. To return to my earlier reference to long inspections of greeting cards, what Harrison does here is to enact, to dramatise, to perform the feelings we inarticulately wish to express in sending the greetings or postcard to one who is truly loved but one, alas, who in this case hears or reads no more. (Harrison's art here invokes for me other great sonnets of personal feeling addressed to deceased loved ones such as Milton's 'I saw my late espousèd saint', or Wordsworth's 'Surprised by joy'.) If the reader does not share my high evaluation, I would nevertheless hope that I have written enough to at least help any reader understand better the project which has eventuated in this line, as well as something of the actualities (rather than prejudices) surrounding clichéd expression in English.

Harrison's Later Work

Though the reputation has stuck, there is not so much cliché in Harrison's more recently published work. This reinforces my argument that cliché in the 'School for Eloquence' sonnets is not a careless weakness, but a deliberate and thoroughly motivated strategy, informed by a full and conscious awareness on the part of the poet of what he was doing, and how provocative it would be considered in some more conservative poetic quarters. It was a specific strategy for a specific kind of writing, but because of its noticeability critics now look for it everywhere. In fact it has to be said that some of the later Harrison is pedestrian and unconvincing and can indeed slip into an insufficiently motivated use of cliché. This happens perhaps particularly in the more public work, for TV or film, where accessibility and fluent catchiness for a mass audience, attuned to cliché and creativity in advertising and chat show, will always pose artistic dilemmas, but where, more positively, a poet like Harrison can at least reach potentially millions, whereas the slim volume of verse is never going to be perused by more than a select few thousand. At the same time, serious poetry first published in newspapers ('A Cold Coming', 1991, a response to the Gulf War, for example) generally avoids cliché in favour of more conventional poetic modes. Here the criticism has generally been of the inappropriately glib tone conveyed by rhyming couplets more than the everyday language. Byronic satiric modes may be inappropriate to the scale of twentieth century abominations, but that is the subject for another essay.

As brief example, 'Initial Illumination' is one such public poem, published in *The Guardian*, March 5, 1991, another response to the Gulf War and interestingly sharing a title word with the sonnet discussed above. This poem again explores different kinds of 'illumination', though this time including those of incendiary bombs being dropped on civilians in Baghdad. There are fairly flat narrative passages, ('off to St Andrew's to record a reading'), but clearly identifiable clichés are less obvious. Most significantly, where clichés seem to occur, they are now used to dismiss the US military, politicians, and their allies (including Britain): 'raiders gung-ho for booty', or 'the word of God *much bandied by George Bush*'(my italics). At best there is a kind of pathos in 'the Baghdad cock who was betrayed/ by bombs into believing *day was dawning*' (my italics). Clearly these clichés, if such they are, have nothing like the resonance of the earlier 'Illumination', and in fact can more justifiably be criticised. The use is still deliberate, it seems, but less well motivated and so less effective. The device is in any case less pervasively used.

Conclusion

I mentioned Bakhtin earlier in discussing Harrison's poetry. In my opinion Bakhtin offers the best stylistic approach to understanding Harrison's poetry (cf. Byrne 1998; also Geyer-Ryan 1989, Wales 1989). Here if ever is a literary use of language which incorporates the everyday language of ordinary people but inflects it anew for the purposes of poetic creativity, fully aware of the tensions and the wider cultural issues any use of language invokes. My title refers to 'Creativity', as well as 'Cliché. Some readers may feel I have written convincingly on cliché but not yet properly addressed the other key term of my title. The Bakhtinian point I have been trying to make, however, is that we cannot understand the one without the other, Literature depends on literature, as the poetic depends on the everyday. These are not mutually exclusive categories or qualities, but mutually defining. It has often been observed that the totally original utterance or text (if such a thing is imaginable) would be incomprehensible. Similarly, the over-familiar escapes our attention. To appreciate fully what it is we require from poetry, and what Harrison gives us through his exploitation of cliché in a poem like 'Illuminations I', we need to turn to another early twentieth century Russian theorist of the literary, Victor Shklovsky. 'People who live by the sea,' Shklovsky famously remarked, 'no longer hear the waves.'

Art exists that one may recover the sensation of life; it exists to make one feel things, to make the stone *stony*. The purpose of art is to impart the sensation of things as they are perceived and not as they are known. (Shklovsky 1917:)

The clichés we live by are not meaningless, but neither is their full meaningfulness easily perceived in everyday interaction. Poetry can help us see and hear the full meaningfulness of these clichés and the experiences they represent in a new light, a new Illumination.

NOTES

[1] Harrison has spoken in interview of 'one of my culture heroes, the comedian 'Professor' Leon Cortez, who offered his own cockneyfications of Shakespeare, reducing the high-flown poetry of kings to an earthy demotic.' (Astley (ed.) 1991: 185).

REFERENCES

Altick, R.D. 1957. *The English Common Reader. A Social History of the Mass Reading Public 1800-1900.* Chicago and London: University of Chicago Press.

Astley, N. (ed.). 1991. *Bloodaxe Critical Anthologies 1: Tony Harrison.* Newcastle upon Tyne: Bloodaxe Books.

Bailey, P. 1994. 'Conspiracies of Meaning: Music Hall and the Knowingness of Popular Culture.' *Past and Present.* 144: 138-170.

Benjamin, W. 1936/ 1973. 'The Work of Art in the Age of Mechanical Reproduction.' In Hannah Arendt (ed.) *Illuminations.* trs, H. Zohn. London: Fontana/Collins.

Byrne, S. 1998. *H, V and O: Tony Harrison's Poetry* Oxford

Carter, R. 1987. *Vocabulary. Applied Linguistic Perspectives.* London: Allen and Unwin.

Coulmas, Florian. 1981. *Conversational Routine. Explorations in Standardized Communication Situations and Prepatterned Speech.* The Hague: Mouton.

Drew, P. and Holt, E. 1988. 'Complainable Matters: The Use of Idiomatic Expressions in Making Complaints.' *Social Problems.* 35 (4): 398-417.

Fowler, H.W. 1965/ 1983. *A Dictionary of Modern English Usage.* 2nd edition revised by E. Gowers. Oxford and New York: Oxford University Press.

Geyer-Ryan. H. 1989. 'Heteroglossia in the Poetry of Bertolt Brecht and Tony Harrison.' In van Peer, W. (ed.). *The Taming of the Text. Explorations in Language, Literature and Culture.* London and New York: Routledge, pp. 193-221.

Halliday, M.A.K. 1978. 'Antilanguages'. In *Language as Social Semiotic. The social interpretation of language and meaning,* London: Arnold, Ch.9.

Harrison, T. 1987. *Selected Poems.* London: Penguin.

Hebert, H. 1985. [Interview with Tony Harrison]. 'Stage Guardian', in *The Guardian,* 18 Jan. 1985, p. 13.

Jakobson, R. 1960/ 1987. 'Linguistics and Poetics. In K. Pomorska and S. Rudy (eds.) *Roman Jakobson. Language in Literature.* Cambridge, MA: Harvard University Press, pp. 62-94.

Kirkpatrick. B. 1996. *Dictionary of Clichés.* London: Bloomsbury.

Lakoff, G. and Turner, M. 1989. *More Than Cool Reason: A Field Guide to Poetic Metaphor.* Chicago and London: University of Chicago Press.

Lynch, D. 1998. *The Economy of Character. Novels, Market Culture, and the Business of Inner Meaning.* Chicago and London: University of Chicago Press.

Monroe, Jonathan. 1990. 'Idiom and Cliché in T.S. Eliot and John Ashbery.' *Contemporary Literature.* 31 (1): 17-35.

Moon, R. 1998. *Fixed Expressions and Idioms in English. A Corpus-Based Approach.* Oxford: Clarendon Press.

Obelkevich, James. 1987. 'Proverbs and Social History.' In: Peter Burke and Roy Porter (eds.). *The Social History of Language.* Cambridge: Cambridge University Press, 43-72.

Orwell, George. 1946. 'Politics and the English Language.' In: *Inside the Whale and Other Essays.* London: Penguin.

Partridge, E. 1940. *A Dictionary of Cliches.* Oxford

Ricks, C. 1993. *Beckett's Dying Words. The Clarendon Lectures 1990.* Oxford: Oxford University Press.

Schegloff, E.A. and Sacks. H. 1973. 'Opening up Closings.' *Semiotica* 8: 289-327.

Shklovsky, V. 1917. 'Art as Technique.' Translated in Lemon, L. and Reis, M.J. (eds.). *Russian Formalist Criticism.* Lincoln: University of Nebraska Press.

Smith, B.H. 1968. *Poetic Closure. A Study of How Poems End.* Chicago and London: University of Chicago Press.

Stubbs, M. 1983. *Discourse Analysis. The Sociolinguistic Analysis of Natural Language.* Oxford. Blackwell.

Wales, K. 1989. In van Peer, W. (ed.). *The Taming of the Text. Explorations in Language, Literature and Culture.* London and New York: Routledge, pp. 176-192.

Watson, J.R. 'Clichés and Common Speech in Philip Larkin's Poetry.' *Critical Survey.* 1 (2): 149-156.

Zijderveld, A.C. 1979. *On Clichés. The Superstructure of Meaning by Function in Modernity.* London: Routledge and Kegan Paul.

Point of View and the Reader in the Poetry of Carol Ann Duffy

Lesley Jeffries

I. Introduction

1.1 Character, context and voices

Carol Ann Duffy's poetry seems to find a way of being accessible and yet challenging and thought-provoking too. It manages to combine humour with serious comment and uses a variety of forms to great effect. As a linguist, what interests me about poetry is how the language makes the poem work. In the case of Duffy's poems, my overwhelming feeling is that they draw me in as a reader and I feel part of them whether or not they are addressed to me and whether they are apparently using the poet's own voice or are speaking the words of a fictional or non-fictional character.

In this investigation, I hope to demonstrate that my feeling of being drawn into Carol Ann Duffy's poems relies at least as much on the poetic strategies she uses as on the fact that I'm roughly the same age and background as her. The arguments I make here are based on a detailed examination of all of the poems in the *Selected Poems* (1994). I chose this text on the assumption that the selection would be largely representative of Duffy's poetry as a whole.

Duffy is well known for using a wide variety of 'voices' in her poems and these range from contemporary disaffected youths and equally disillusioned teachers to historical and hypothetical characters, such as the neighbours of Joseph and Mary, the wives of Aesop, Lazarus and Midas and the Captain of the 1964 Top of the Form team. There are also times when Duffy takes the voice of animals and birds, such as in 'The Dolphins' and 'Dies Natalis', but these are not so common.

There are almost as many poems in the *Selected Poems* which do not use a voice that is identifiably that of a character. This is not to say that these poems should necessarily be attributed to Duffy's voice, although I would suggest that readers tend to assume that poems are in the poet's voice in the absence of clues to the contrary. One of the claims of this paper is that dividing the work into those poems which seem to be Duffy speaking and those which have a 'voice' does not throw any light on the stylistic question of what Duffy is doing to draw the reader in. We will return to this issue in the conclusion.

1.2 Deixis

In wrestling with the question of reader-involvement, I tried to apply to the poems some of the techniques of stylistics that have been developed with prose fiction in mind. In particular I attempted to work out which features of what is known as 'point of view' were significant in Duffy's poetry. Whilst features of transitivity, modality and speech and thought representation (see Simpson 1993) were noteworthy in some of the poems, it seemed to be the spatial, temporal and personal point of view that showed a consistently interesting pattern throughout the *Selected Poems*. Together, these aspects of point of view are often known as 'deixis' by linguists and the term refers to features of language that depend for their meaning on the speaker's positioning, either vis-à-vis the surroundings or with respect to other people.

The easiest way to describe deixis is by using the example of personal pronouns in English. There is a stage when children are learning the language when adults tend, quite naturally, to talk about themselves and the baby in the third person:

> Mummy's going downstairs now. Janie go to sleep, there's a good girl.

The child responds by learning to use third person forms, even to people in the room:

> Mummy come. Janie want biscuit.

What the adults are instinctively recognising is the difficulty of learning what the words 'I' and 'you' mean, because unlike proper names they change their reference, depending on who is speaking. If we alter the invented examples above to include first and second person pronouns, we can see that the meaning of 'I' changes from 'Mummy' to 'Janie' and the meaning of 'you' changes from Janie to Mummy:

> I'm going downstairs now. You go to sleep, there's a good girl.

> You come. I want a biscuit.

There are certain areas of English vocabulary, then, where the meaning of the words is not fixed but varies in this way with the perspective of the speaker. Spatial positioning in relation to the speaker is conveyed by adverbs like 'here' and 'there' and more subtly also by the demonstrative pronouns 'this', 'these', 'that' and 'those'. In the following examples, we imagine the speaker being near to (possibly holding) the flowers when they are preceded by 'these' and pointing to them at the other side of the room when they are preceded by 'those':

> Put *these* flowers in water will you?

> Put *those* flowers in water will you?

Finally, temporal positioning is conveyed in a number of ways, including verbal tense, but the clearest examples are those adverbs and adverbials which relate to the time of speaking ('now', 'on Tuesday') and those which relate to a past time ('then', 'when'...).

The dimensions of temporal, spatial and personal deixis have in common the fact that at one end they are perceived as 'near' to the speaker and at the other end they are perceived as 'distant' from the speaker. This distinction is labelled by the terms 'proximal' (near) and 'distal' (distant). Clearly the proximity or otherwise is not necessarily physical, but can also be used metaphorically. Thus we are likely to use distal terms to describe something we do not like, but proximal ones for things we admire:

> I must get rid of *those* curtains!

> I want *these* curtains - they're lovely!

1.3 Drawing in the reader
The claim that I want to make in this paper is that in her poems

Carol Ann Duffy exploits the deictic systems of English in a number of ways that enable the reader to take up a position in relation to the substance of the poems, irrespective of whether or not the reader is being addressed or included directly.

It is part of my argument that the readers of poetry (or indeed, prose) are likely to identify with the speaker's deictic position and that consequently, high levels of proximal deixis indicate a close relationship between the speaker's position and that of the reader.

As well as enticing her readers into the 'here and now', Duffy plays with our expectations of the difference between proximal and distal deixis in such a way that the differences start to disappear and we no longer know whether we are 'here' or 'there', in the present, past or future, or even who we are in relation to the 'I' and 'you' of the poems.

2. Here and There

2.1 Exile
One of Duffy's themes, particularly in poems drawn from *The Other Country*, is that of exile. As an early emigrant from Scotland she is conscious of the childhood traumas of displacement:

> We came from our own country in a red room
> ['Originally': 65]

Even here, in the poem dealing most directly with her own sense of loss of identity, she uses a proximal verb, 'came', to locate herself in the new country. The effect on the reader is that we locate ourselves with Duffy in the new country. Another poem with a similar theme, 'In Your Mind', deals with the experience of immigrants to England, and ends with the character waking from a daydream:

> For a moment
> you are there, in the other country, knowing its name.
> And then a desk. A newspaper. A window. English rain.
> ['In Your Mind': 89]

The 'other country', in this extract is placed by a distal adverb, 'there', whilst the new place dawns on the daydreamer gradually as her/his gaze moves from the desk up and out of the window to see the characteristic feature of English weather: the rain.

2.1 Locating the narrator

The great majority of the poems in the *Selected Poems* use proximal deixis to locate the narrator, whether or not that narrator is, or seems to be, Carol Ann Duffy. Thus the English teacher in 'Head of English' talks to the poet and we feel as though we are with them. This is partly achieved by the proximal 'here':

> Thank you
> very much for coming here today.
> ['Head of English': 8]

Similarly in 'Warming her Pearls', the maid who is in love with her mistress lies in bed and uses proximal adverb 'here', drawing the reader into close contact with her feelings:

> slipping naked into bed, the way
>
> she always does . . . And I lie here awake,
> ['Warming her Pearls': 60]

Other poems occasionally use distal deixis, but usually only to emphasise the spatial positioning of the speaker at the centre of the poem's focus. Thus the poem 'Away and See' repeats the phrase of the title to encourage the addressee of the poem to travel, to experience life:

> Away and see an ocean suck at a boiled sun
> ['Away and See': 107]

The effect of the word 'away' is that, by indicating movement away from the speaker's position, it re-emphasises the centrality of the speaker. This might be one reason why this poem does not seem to be harshly saying goodbye, but rather implies that the traveller will return but needs to spend some time away.

Another example of distal deixis which seems to ironically underline the 'here', rather than 'there', comes from 'Small Female Skull':

> Downstairs they will think I have lost my mind
> ['Small Female Skull': 109]

This poem takes place in a bathroom where the speaker is trying to recover from a hangover. The use of 'Downstairs' gives us the speaker's perspective and places us in the bathroom with the speaker, in order to see the ground floor as being 'downstairs'. To this extent, despite being distal, it works to draw us into the poem.

In some places, Duffy makes conscious use of the differences in deixis between different speakers' perspectives. If two speakers are in the same place, their 'here' is the same, but if one is native to that place and one is an immigrant, the words 'here' and 'there' take on different connotations:

> It's all them
> coming over here to work

> There was much more room to play than here in London
> ['Comprehensive': 5]

The first speaker is Wayne who supports the National Front, the second is Masjid who remembers families facing Mecca. The sense of 'here' being alien and therefore more distal than 'there' for a displaced person is stronger as a result of the juxtaposition of the two viewpoints.

The last example begins to show how Duffy can subvert the certainties of deixis so that we begin to see how the place where you are physically might seem rather distant. The poem concerned, 'Comprehensive', finishes with another immigrant emphasising these unreal feelings of being a new immigrant:

> At first I felt as if I was dreaming, but I wasn't.
> Everything I saw was true.
> ['Comprehensive': 6]

2.1 Playing with place

Another way in which Duffy exploits our understanding of spatial deixis is in the poem 'The Dolphins', where the voice of the poem is one of two dolphins in captivity who is trying to make sense of the limited amount of water s/he has to swim in. The world is defined in the poem as 'what you swim in' and in this case it is a very small world:

> Outside this world you cannot breathe for long.
> ['The Dolphins': 25]

It is a proximal demonstrative, 'this', which simultaneously focuses the reader on the pool where the dolphins are kept and by implied contrast suggests that there might be other worlds too. The increased anxiety of knowing that the world you are trapped in is not the whole story is underlined in the following line:

> We have found no truth in these waters,
> ['The Dolphins': 25]

Here, again, a proximal demonstrative, 'these', brings the reader into the water with the dolphins, but the reference to truth indicates that there must be other waters where such a thing might be found.

3. Now and Then

3.1 Present and past narratives

About half of the poems in the *Selected Poems* have a largely present tense orientation, although there are also a considerable number which use a fairly conventional past tense narrative approach, such as we see in the opening poem, 'Girl Talking':

> On our Eid day my cousin was sent to
> the village. Something happened. We think it was pain.
> [′Girl Talking': 3]

There is a complicated relationship between tense and time in English, but it is generally true to say that a narrative told in the present tense will involve the reader more directly because it appears to be happening, as in a film, as the narrative progresses. This is illustrated by the poem called 'Education for Leisure' where the speaker decides to kill something at the beginning of the poem and finds the first victim in the second stanza:

> I squash a fly against the window with my thumb.
> ['Education for Leisure': 11]

In the next stanza the goldfish is poured away and the poem ends by threatening us:

> The pavements glitter suddenly. I touch your arm.

I will look at the impact of the second person pronoun, 'your', in the next section. Here it is worth noting that the deictic effect of the present tense narrative is to place us (the readers) at the temporal moment when each successive part of the story happens. This allows the force of the final line to be fully felt, since we have been following the story as it unfolds, albeit assuming that we were simply onlookers, rather than participants, until that final chilling sentence.

As with the spatial deixis, the temporal markers apart from verbal tense are overwhelmingly proximal in the majority of these poems. Like the spatial deixis, this has the effect of making the reader 'present' in the time zone when the poem takes place. 'Head of English', for example, specifies that 'Today we have a poet in the class' and 'Moments of Grace' talks of 'These days' and 'Now I smell you peeling an orange in the other room'.

One or two poems create a time sequence using adverbs and tenses to tell a tale of what was past, what is happening 'now' and what the future will hold. Perhaps the most effective one is 'Brothers' which begins by looking back to childhood:

> *Once*, I slept in a bed with these four men
> ['Brothers': 101]

Notice that the proximal deixis of 'these' makes us feel that we are in a room with the five people concerned. The temporal references move through two present time phrases, 'even now' and 'Occasionally' and end with a prediction about the future:

> *One day*
> I shall pay for a box and watch them shoulder it.
> ['Brothers': 101]

Whilst it is now some time since this poem was written, the 'now' of the poem remains, long after the actual present time referred to has passed. Thus we re-enter the moment each time we read the poem.

3.2 Generic narratives

One of the most common types of temporal focus in Duffy's poems is what I will call generic narratives. These are stories which are told through the second person indefinite, 'you', which is interpreted as meaning 'one', i.e., anyone or everyone.

I will examine the complications of this use of the second person in Section 4, but here it is worth illustrating the temporal relevance of such narratives. One of the poems mentioned in connection with exile and immigration was 'In Your Mind'. This poem is written as a generic narrative, and as well as its capacity to challenge the deixis of place which we have already seen, it opens with a line that questions the distinction between past and future time:

> The other country, is it anticipated or half-remembered?
> ['In Your Mind': 89]

This direct questioning of one of the practical certainties of life, that time is linear, undermines the reader's notion of existing in a certain time zone, and this adds to the unsettling effect of the poem, which is, after all, about displacement and migration. The next extract from the same poem illustrates the generic narrative:

> and in your mind
> you put aside your work and head for the airport
> with a credit card and a warm coat you will leave
> on the plane.
> ['In Your Mind': 89]

The details of the story, such as the coat that is left behind, serve to make it more vivid and there is a sense that there might well be a real story behind the poem. However, the consistent use of 'you' leads the reader to a more generic reading which in turn allows for an empathetic identification with the protagonist: whether or not *you*, the reader, have ever been in exile in this way.

3.3 *Playing with time*

One of the poems in which Duffy plays with temporal deixis is 'Shooting Stars'. This poem describes one of the horrors of the Holocaust: Jewish people being stood next to an open mass grave and shot one by one. It opens apparently as a present tense narrative:

> After I no longer speak they break our fingers
> to salvage my wedding ring.
> ['Shooting Stars': 23]

Much of the poem which follows is then told as a straightforward past tense narrative as in 'You waited for the bullet' or 'My bare feet felt the earth'. However, this story is interspersed with general exhortations to 'Remember', with statements locating the temporal focus in the present such as 'Only a matter of days separate / this from acts of torture now' and with other generalisations relating to 'then', but linked by their present tense to similar acts now:

> After immense suffering someone takes tea on the lawn.
> After the terrible moans a boy washes his uniform.

Because of the level of detail in the past tense narrative, the reader is led to read these as an extension of that story. The change in tense, however, alerts us to the fact that these kinds of everyday activity in the face of enormous evil are repeated in the world of the present too.

4. Me, You and Them

I have already asserted that the difference of effect between poems written in Duffy's own voice and those in other voices is not very great as far as reader involvement is concerned. This statement requires supporting evidence from the poems. It is also revealing to consider in more detail the whole question of the pronouns used in her poems and more importantly who the speakers and addressees appear to be.

4.1 Third person narratives

In deictic terms, as I have already explained, 'I' and 'you' represent proximal and distal deixis respectively. A further distancing is achieved by using the third person to talk to and about other people, since it implies that they are not present, or at least are not intended to be the addressee(s) of the poem. In fact, Duffy uses third person narratives very rarely in the *Selected Poems*, there being a total of only seven poems (out of seventy four) which could be said to be written in a largely third person mode. These include poems such as 'A Healthy Meal', in which the protagonists are not named, but described in general terms, and therefore could be read as generic:

> The gourmet tastes the secret dreams of cows
> ['A Healthy Meal': 27]

One or two poems actually seem to tell a story of a particular character, but these do not seem to me to be typical of Duffy's work and in particular differ from those equally detailed stories of equally individual characters which are found in the first and second person narratives. As an example, here are two lines from 'Eley's Bullet':

> At ten, Eley came into the bedroom with drinks.
> She was combing her hair at the mirror.
> ['Eley's Bullet': 80]

4.2 First person narratives
It would be simplistic to say that the reader feels involved as a result of Duffy's using mostly first person structures in her poems. There could be a difference between her own and other voices, even though the first person is used for both. There might also be a difference of involvement depending on whether there is an explicit addressee and whether she or he is a specified character, or the reader.

Many of the poems written in 'other' voices have no explicit 'you' and yet the spoken style of the language, using colloquialisms and conversational asides, for example, leads the reader to construct an implied audience to whom the poem is addressed directly. One example of this type of poem is 'Descendants', where the style is casual throughout and sounds as though it would be spoken:

> And she started, didn't she.
> Tears all over her lovely blotchy purple face. It got to me.
> ['Descendants': 75]

Whilst in this poem dealing with the survivors of nuclear holocaust we are only vaguely aware that there is someone who is being spoken to, there are other poems which indicate that the text is really part of a longer conversation. 'Stealing' opens and closes with a question, the first one sounding like a repeated question which has already been spoken by the person being addressed:

> The most unusual thing I ever stole? A snowman.
> ['Stealing': 49]

This impression is not explicitly confirmed until the last line of the poem where another question, this time emanating from the speaker, pulls the reader up short:

> You don't understand a word I'm saying, do you?
> ['Stealing': 50]

The sudden use of the second person pronoun here allows Duffy to use it both to imply that there is an addressee in the context and to bring the reader in as an additional addressee. The reader is thereby challenged as to whether she or he has indeed understood the content and force of the poem.

Whilst the shadowy presence of an addressee gives life and vibrancy to the poem, there is another group of poems with specific voices which are also more specific as to the addressee. These include 'The Biographer' which addresses the dead person whose biography is being written:

> I'm a passionate man
> with a big advance
> who's loved your work since he was a boy;
> ['The Biographer': 123]

The intimacy of a confessional-style poem to a dead person allows the reader to take a semi-voyeuristic role in eavesdropping on the monologue. This is one of Duffy's techniques of drawing the reader in, since the observation of private thoughts/conversations is one of the most compelling of human activities. A similar process operates in the poems concerned with illicit love such as 'Telegrams' and 'Correspondents', from which the following is taken:

> I have called your name over and over in my head
> at the point your fiction brings me to.
> ['Correspondents': 56]

In these poems, as in all love poems, the reader tends to identify with the object of the poem, whether or not the details of the person concerned fit the reader her/himself. Some of Duffy's love poems are more clearly in her own voice and the effect of reader-identification with the 'you' of the poem is intensified by the sparser detail about the lover, who often seems to be absent, as in this extract from the opening of 'Miles Away':

> I want you and you are not here. I pause
> in this garden, breathing the colour thought is

before language into still air.
['Miles Away': 62]

Here, Duffy merges the distant place where the lover is with the speaker's own situation in the time-honoured way, by thinking hard about her and in a sense also merging their identities by holding her inside her head:

I hold you closer, miles away,
['Miles Away': 62]

Here we begin to see two of the deictic dimensions (space and person) being dispensed with, or perhaps more accurately 'overcome', by the strength of love.

Whilst we may put ourselves in the position of a loved one in any love poem, since it is nice to think about someone writing a poem about us, there are some Duffy poems that use the second person very clearly to directly address the reader. Sometimes this seems to play with notions of authorship and reader power, as in 'Talent' where Duffy taunts the reader when she describes a tightrope walker. She acknowledges the fact that writers and readers create meaning jointly in 'He holds our breath' where the plural possessive adjective 'our' implies a writer and reader working in harmony. However, the tension between the two is illustrated as Duffy challenges us with 'You want him to fall, don't you?'. She doesn't let him fall.

This is fun; but more startling, and therefore more moving, are the moments when the reader is suddenly addressed in the midst of a poem which has not apparently addressed you until that moment. This happens in 'Shooting Stars', the poem commemorating Jewish victims of the Nazi holocaust. The poem changes deictic focus a number of times, and is 'spoken' from the point of view of one of the victims:

After I no longer speak, they break our fingers
['Shooting Stars': 23]

At times there seems to be another addressee, also present at the graveside, when the speaker says 'You would not look at me'. However, the reader feels more drawn in to the story as the imperative 'Remember' is repeated in the second stanza, the implicit 'you' of the command inevitably referring to people who live after that time, including the reader. The poem continues with another shocking piece of narrative in the past tense which allows the reader temporarily to distance her/himself from the atrocious revelations. And then the third stanza opens with a question that seems to stare out of the page and ask the reader directly:

> How would *you* prepare to die, on a perfect April evening
> with young men gossiping and smoking by the graves?
> ['Shooting Stars': 23]

4.3 Second person narratives

I have already introduced the notion of second person narratives (section 3.2), but here I would like to illustrate in more detail how the use of 'you' as the main subject of a story will cause the reader to identify more closely with the action, at the same time as suspecting that the detail of the story belongs to a particular person, sometimes to Duffy herself.

These poems mostly lack any other 'person', although there may be one or two incidental third person characters who crop up. There is certainly not usually a mixture of first person and second person protagonists in one poem. 'I Remember Me' is a poem about faces and identity and uses the second person to generalise about recognition and people's faces:

> Everyone
> you meet is telling wordless barefaced truths.
> ['I Remember Me': 12]

This could have been written in the first person as a real but somewhat bizarre experience, leading the reader to distance her/himself from any identification with the speaker, particularly if the past tense is also used to create further distal deixis:

> Everyone
> I met was telling wordless barefaced truths.

When Duffy finishes the poem with an event which sounds like a real, one-off experience, we are ready to interpret her words in terms relevant to ourselves, whatever our own experience:

> Mostly your lover passes
> in the rain and does not know you when you speak.
>   ['I Remember Me': 12]

Clearly the effect of changing this to the first person, past tense version would be to limit the occurrence to an incident rather than enabling it to be generalised to mean something more about recognition and human relationships.

5. Conclusion

My starting point with this essay was to try and work out from a stylistic perspective why Carol Ann Duffy's poems seemed to draw me, as a reader, into their worlds, even though many of them related places, times and experiences which were not familiar to me. Increasingly it seemed that my findings were pointing towards a very subtle and quite varied exploitation of a number of deictic dimensions in English. These could be used 'straightforwardly' by emphasising proximal deixis of place, time or person, but were also very often concerned with challenging the very basis on which deictic opposition rests. Thus the distinctions in Duffy's poems between 'there' and 'here', between 'me' and 'you' and between the past and the future are repeatedly blurred and their identities made to fluctuate. The result for the reader, I would claim, is that by different means we are time and again drawn into the centre of the poem. Sometimes we are addressed directly, sometimes the generic nature of the narrative seems to be all-inclusive. At times we know that we are 'here' or 'now', but just as we have identified the physical context or time-zone of the poem, it may be changed and we find ourselves re-orienting to a new focus.

REFERENCES
Duffy, Carol Ann, *Selected Poems*, Penguin 1994
Simpson, P., *Language, Ideology and Point of View*, Routledge 1993

Gunn's Family of Man in 'The Hug'

Martin Dodsworth

The opening poem of *The Man with Night Sweats* (1992) deserves to figure in any anthology of twentieth-century poetry in English. The excellence of 'The Hug' is intrinsic to it, a matter of craft and sure artistry, but it is also bound into a complex dialogue with the poet's own works and with the works of others in the past. I want to argue something of the poem's combination of grace and depth and something, too, of its generosity of spirit.

Like Thom Gunn's earliest work 'The Hug' is a rhyming poem. But its rhyme has little in common with the crispness of *Fighting Terms*. In this poem sound works not in the cause of rhetorical pointedness but to suggest a more diffuse harmoniousness. The mood is different, and part of the difference lies in the way lines of varying length are bound together unpredictably with full rhymes that also chime with other rhymes. Take the poem's opening;

> It was your birthday, we had drunk and dined
> Half of the night with our old friend
> Who'd showed us in the end
> To a bed I reached in one drunk stride.
> Already I lay snug,
> And drowsy with the wine dozed on one side.

'Dined' does not find its pair in rhyme until the next line after this quotation ends, but you would not necessarily be aware of that because the rhymes 'end' and 'friend' chime with 'dined' in their final consonants, whilst 'stride' and 'side', also full rhymes, chime with it in the vowel sound. The result is a kind of after-dinner sonorousness that sets the tone of the poem. Technique is without flaw here, as the insouciant expansion and contraction of the line is kept from agitation by the easy unreeling of the syntax. Even apparent redundancy has its rightness. That phrase 'in the end' looks slack but goes cheerfully with the poet's fuzzy state of drunkenness, whilst giving value to the fact that 'half the night' has been spent in drinking and dining. The whole effect is one of a relaxed harmony, appropriate to what is being evoked, a birthday celebration whose allowance of surprise and spontaneity is reflected in the unpredictable way the lines change in length.

There is nothing archaic about it, though; the diction is plain and unaffected, but undeniably of the twentieth century. Yet in its grace of form the poem looks back to the seventeenth century. The structure of varied rhyme and line-length recalls, for example, the inventiveness of Herbert in 'The Collar', a very, perhaps significantly, different sort of poem. A phrase from Herrick – 'wild civility' – readily comes to mind as a description of the fluently erratic development of the poem's drunken opening. And the theme, a celebration of friendship, is one most associated with Herrick's master, Ben Jonson, whose work Gunn specially admires. The point is not that doings in contemporary California are given an antique veneer. Insofar as the seventeenth century is alluded to here it is because it is felt to be still alive, still to be decently enjoyed; the allusion rests lightly on what is alluded to because there is no effort to bring the whole of that century's thought and practice into the poem. All that happens is that friendship, celebration and that valuation of the particular moment which is also implicit in Herbert's form are deftly signalled as having historical weight. They count now in the way they have for the last four hundred years. The poet is not interested in metaphysics or seventeenth-century spirituality but in establishing with minimum fuss, indeed with grace, that what he finds important now has always, or at least for a long time, been seen like that. Since what he is talking about is the long-disputed values of a gay relationship, this allusive use of form, integral to the poem, has exceptional power.

The poem's subject is an intimate kind of friendship:

> I dozed, I slept. My sleep broke on a hug,
>   Suddenly, from behind,
> In which the full length of our bodies pressed:
>   Your instep to my heel,
>   My shoulder-blades against your chest.

This friendship has a physical basis; it insists, as the verse insists, on the body – instep, heel, shoulder-blades, chest. In the context of its allusive form this embrace may be contrasted with another, this time heterosexual, in a poem from the sixteenth century. One of Wyatt's most famous poems, 'They flee from me that sometime did me seek', has at its heart a memory of a different kind of hug, when 'she me caught in her arms long and small'. 'It was no dream: I lay broad waking', but it feels like dream all the same, because the erotic charge is of seduction, of fantasy fulfilled ('And softly said, "Dear heart, how like you this?"') and then disappointed. In Gunn, 'the full length of our bodies pressed' is matter-of-fact, not an erotic tease (not even the thought that this might be a dream is possible), and there is neither doubt nor disappointment but an acknowledgement of 'the stay' of the partner's embrace. Wyatt's poem is about 'love' as a claim to proprietorship; in it, the poet is frustrated by his inability to control the women who once came 'stalking in his chamber' like tame animals. Gunn's poem by contrast is about a form of freedom, a freedom to which touch is crucial. He has written about this before, in the poem called 'Touch', where physical contact leads to the liberties of shared consciousness:

> is it
> my own warmth surfacing
> or the ferment of your whole
> body that in darkness beneath
> the cover is stealing

The uncertainty about what is being felt when one body touches another enlarges to become a

> dark
> enclosing cocoon round
> ourselves alone, dark
> wide realm where we
> walk with everyone.

The difference between 'The Hug' and 'Touch' is a matter of confidence and security. The nervous balance of 'ourselves alone' and 'everyone' in the lines just quoted relates to the emphasis on darkness in the vision of freedom that 'Touch' embodies. It is as though the release that touch brings with it is too good to be believed – that wide realm, though populated by everyone, still feels, in its darkness, a lonely sort of place. In 'The Hug', on the other hand, darkness is not a significant feature and the couple in their embrace are not surrounded by a sense of their own isolation. They have after all been celebrating with a friend who puts them up for the night.

In neither of these two poems does the sex (or identity) of the partner become an issue. In 'Touch' the reason seems to be that Gunn was not yet ready to make his sexuality part of public knowledge; in 'The Hug' the sexuality is implicit from what is explicit elsewhere in the whole volume of which it is part, as well as from the use of the phrase 'your chest', and the point of the poem's reticence seems to be to say that sexual orientation is not the only thing that matters, or that to have one sexual orientation or another (or another or another) is so commonplace that its precise nature need not be dwelt on.

In fact, 'The Hug' is a climactic poem for Gunn; it relates, for example, to those poems of isolated consciousness, 'Misanthropos' and 'Jack Straw's Castle', which have a central position in his *oeuvre*. The sense of isolation is important right from the start; the self does not wish to be revealed: 'Even in bed I pose'. 'La Prisonnière' ('Now I will shut you in a box / With massive sides and a lid that locks') is plainly about this hidden self, and the hiding is related, via the title of the fifth volume of Proust's *A la Recherche,* to homosexuality. In the pre-Wolfenden years a disinclination to be identified at large as gay was natural, but in Gunn the consequences, to judge by *Fighting Terms,* went deep. The significance of touch in 'Touch' is that it entails a melting away of 'the black frost / of outsideness'. The pose is abandoned, the mask is dropped and fears like his partner's 'dreamed pogrom' can be faced in the 'dark / wide realm'. In 'The Hug' there is no pose, no mask, and touch has a different quality, not that of a loosening ('What I, now loosened, / sink into …') but of a stay, of a familiarity (or familiality) that confirms the self that is already there. This concern transcends that of sex:

> It was not sex, but I could feel
> The whole strength of your body set,

> Or braced, to mine,
> And locking me to you
> As if we were still twenty-two
> When our grand passion had not yet
> Become familial.

If it was not sex, what was it? The poem does not say, but implies its answer in the set of the strong body and the long journey of the sentence to its final word 'familial'. What is celebrated is the strength of the familial and in this celebration sexuality and difference of sexuality are studiously ignored, because they are here taken to be irrelevant. The lines act out the achievement that this entails in the hesitation of the body's being 'set, / Or braced'. The first term is overlaid by the second, so that the familial relationship is both taken for granted in the inertness of 'set' and worked for in the active virtue of the 'braced' embrace. A similar overlaying is present in the way the 'grand passion' merges into the familial, and this inclusiveness is part of the poem's appeal, for just as it binds a gay experience into everyone else's, so it binds theirs into the gay one.

The point is important, because the poem is not merely personal. The allusions to history depend on its being a living thing, and this is clearest in the case of the, poem's most obvious allusion, to Donne's poem 'The Extasie'. In that poem the lovers' souls are understood to be saying:

> This Extasie doth unperplex
> … and tell us what we love,
> Wee see by this, it was not sexe,
> Wee see, we saw not what did move
> But as all severall soules containe
> Mixture of things, they know not what,
> Love, these mixt soules, doth mixe againe,
> And makes both one, each this and that.

'The Hug' is a twentieth-century, unplatonic version of 'The Extasie'. Its two bodies are not facing each other, as in Donne, and there is not the same self-absorption, but they are as close, and their closeness bears as powerful a meaning. There is a difference of quality. In Donne there is temporary division of body and spirit; the lovers' souls hover somewhere above their bodies:

> And whilst our soules negotiate there,
>   Wee like sepulchrall statues lay...

In Gunn there is no such separation; that 'lock' of two bodies insists on consciousness within the bodies, and sensation from 'Your instep to my heel, / My shoulder-blades against your chest'. His poem is located in an entirely material universe.

The point of the Donne allusion, then, is to put that universe on a footing with Donne's. But there is something more to it than that. 'The Extasie' used to be seen as above all a poem of married love. Sir Herbert Grierson wrote that in his love-poetry Donne

> sets over against the abstract idealism, the sharp dualism of the Middle Ages, a justification of love as a natural passion in the human heart the meaning and end of which is marriage.

Gunn's poem is also a 'justification of love as a natural passion', but it is so outside the context of marriage and in a universe where souls are not distinguished from bodies. It is a kind of appropriation of Donne; it is a bold updating of Donne to apply his words to a gay relationship and, by the use of the word 'familial', to adjust the association of Donne and marriage to it. But then again, the poem implies, it is not. The very fact that the poem's allusiveness comes without sign of strain indicates that.

'The Hug' ends with another exchange with the earlier poem, 'Touch'. That poem is about a kind of Lawrencian lapsing-out of a numbing consciousness into the 'dark / wide realm where / we walk with everyone'. This poem is about passing into a focused consciousness:

> My quick sleep had deleted all
> Of intervening time and place.
>   I only knew
> The stay of your secure firm dry embrace.

Though the speaker is held in that secure embrace, he is free; 'dry' is an important word because it corrects an emphasis in Donne. *His* lovers' hands are 'firmly cimented', but there is nothing stickily adhesive about Gunn's pair, nothing proprietorial about them. His conception of the familial omits the possessive.

'The Hug' is a wonderful poem, beautifully crafted, packed with meaning in itself and in dialogue with other poems. It demonstrates how complex and discriminating a force the poetic urge is in Gunn. Read in relation to the rest of *The Man with Night Sweats* it reveals yet more meanings, yet more claims for the familial. But that is another story.

NOTES

'The Hug' is the first poem in Thom Gunn's *The Man with Night Sweats* (Faber, 1992).

This article was first published in *Agenda*, Vol.37, nos. 2-3 (Autumn-Winter 1999).

Reading for Writing: Simon Armitage

Peter Sansom

This essay looks at three early poems by Armitage, two of them rather briefly, with a view to considering techniques and procedures that we might use in our own writing. It also discusses good practice in composition, and uncovers certain general principles (notably organicism), often with reference to Keats's *Letters*. It's commonly accepted that wide reading and close reading are essential to any writer's development, and this is particularly the case with poetry. We see more clearly what we might do by seeing how others do it.

Nevertheless, though the essay assumes that our writing can only be as good as our reading, there are more important factors than reading, and one in particular. I'm referring to talent, or more specifically imagination and a flair for language. Armitage is prodigiously gifted, though that is not what makes his writing exemplary, why it has so many features we might learn from. I'm not suggesting we take him, or anyone, as a model; there's no merit in sounding like anyone but us; but, paradoxically, it's by attending to others that we find ways of being ourselves. This assertion is not easily proved, though every serious writer thinks it's true, not least Armitage himself; and the basic principle would hardly surprise a musician, for example, or a comedian. 'I don't read,' some young poets say, 'because I don't want to be influenced.' Did anyone ever start a band saying 'I never listen to music'? (Probably, but it wasn't Lennon and McCartney.) And who's going to do stand-up if they've never heard a joke – and probably the same joke – among thousands of others, delivered in dozens of different ways?

Talent is important, but our own talent is no concern of ours; worrying about that shit, as Larkin once said a jazz musician said, don't do us no good. Jeremy Beadle notwithstanding, nobody is naturally unfunny. Some people have the knack of making us laugh, but what distinguishes comedians is that they want, or need, to make us laugh. Also that they're serious about it. Paul Merton's trademark is spontaneity, but we know that he's a walking encyclopedia of comic technique. Prodigiously gifted, but like Armitage he has, as W.S. Graham would say, 'the rarer gift of application'.

'It Ain't What You Do...'

So, I don't mean talent. What is this one thing above all that's more important than reading? It's what Armitage himself talks about in the first poem we'll look at; and he defines it in the poem's title: 'It Ain't What You Do, It's What It Does To You':

> I have not bummed across America
> with a dollar to spare, one pair
> of busted Levi's and a bowie knife.
> I have lived with thieves in Manchester.
>
> I have not padded through the Taj Mahal,
> barefoot, listening to the space between
> each footfall picking up and putting down
> its print against the marble floor. But I
>
> skimmed flat stones across Black Moss on a day
> so still I could hear each set of ripples
> as they crossed. I felt each stone's inertia
> spend itself against the water; then sink.
>
> I have not toyed with a parachute cord
> while perched on the lip of a light aircraft;
> but I held the wobbly head of a boy
> at the day centre, and stroked his fat hands.
>
> And I guess that the tightness in the throat
> and the tiny cascading sensation
> somewhere inside us are both part of that
> sense of something else. That feeling, I mean.

The title explains something crucial to the impulse behind all of Armitage's writing. In this instance, he's taken the old pre-war song, back in the charts in the late eighties (when this poem was written) through Fun Boy Three and Bananarama: 'It ain't what you do, it's the way that you do it/That's what gets results'. First, he draws on contemporary culture – rather than, say, Greek myth – then he overturns the popular sentiment to make his own statement. It's not the way you do it, but what you allow it to do to you. It's not the kind of experience you've undergone – such exotica as visiting the Taj Mahal – but the quality of the experience, how deeply you experience for example skimming stones across a reservoir. Experiencing anything deeply enough will allow you to find the language to convey some of that experience. It's observation, clearly; but more than that it's openness to experience.

Well, where can we learn that? I think we must have it already, or potentially, or we wouldn't want to write poems. My own belief is that writing is a way not just of ordering and making sense of our experience, but actually a means of opening ourselves to experience. We can see that what matters is the way Armitage does it. It's not merely a question of noticing those ripples, or having the language and tools – the poetic devices – to translate them into poetry. Here, it is in the idiomatic language disciplined by form, the strict decasyllabics parcelled into quatrains; and the half- and internal-rhyme, devices pleasing in themselves but also expressive. Stanza three makes its impact partly because of the unforced rightness of the diction: accurate but surprising to say a 'set of ripples' or to talk about 'inertia'; but also because of the crossing of internal rhyme, lines apart, in 'across Black Moss/ …/as they crossed.' And the lovely half-rhyme, 'inertia' and 'water' , whose purpose is to mimic the sense, the rhyme arriving before the end of the measure:

> … as they crossed. I felt each stone's inertia
> spend itself against the water; then sink.

The stone's inertia as it were reaches the semicolon, then drops, like a stone.

Nevertheless, the prime prerequisite is the experience itself, and that needn't be exceptional. It's what you make of it, or more exactly, as Armitage says, what it makes of you: that's what gets results. But what results, the poem implicitly asks, are we looking for?

'Greenhouse'

About this poem, Armitage has said, 'three on the face of it contradictory things: that it's about a greenhouse, that it's a love poem, and that it's to my father'.

Greenhouse

It's gone to seed now; each loose pane pitted
with lichen like the walls of a fish tank,
the soffits lagged with a fur of cobwebs.
I burst in the other day; kicked the door
out of its warped frame, stood in the green light
among nine years of unnatural growth
and thought back to the morning we built it.
We used the old sash windows from the house,
held them flat with leather gloves, steadied them
down the path. I remember that journey:
you out in front, unsure of your footing
on the damp stones, and me behind counting
each of your steps through our cargo of glass.

Some nights I'd watch from my bedroom window
as you arrived home late from a concert,
and leaving the headlights on to guide you
waded into the black of the garden.
I'd wait, straining for the sound of the hasp
or guess your distance by the sparkle
of a cuff link. When you disturbed them
the seeds of rose-bay willow-herbs lifted
like air bubbles into the beam of light.
Then you'd emerge, a hoard of tomatoes
swelling the lap of your luminous shirt;
and caught in the blur of double glazing
your perfect ghost, just one step behind you.

The first significance for anyone new to writing is just this: that the poet has written about something abstract – the relationship between father and son – through description. He doesn't trouble to explain what it meant to him, their making the greenhouse together that day, or why some nights he'd watch his dad from his window: the almost loving attention to detail ('straining for the sound of the hasp'; 'the sparkle/of a cuff link') says enough. Armitage gets the literal detail right, and allows the figurative to speak through it. It is not all neutral description, however, and from the opening words one theme of the poem is made plain: 'It's gone to seed now', a phrase that captures the reader's attention because it's an odd, though apt, thing to say of a greenhouse past its best. This, pretty much, is that theme: 'gone to seed' means ceasing to flower as the seed begins to grow, and it describes the father as the son comes into his own, begins as it were to blossom. It is a loving poem, but it's clear-eyed about this. Or maybe we feel the greenhouse represents only the relationship, that the days of the son as a sort of apprentice are numbered and that father and son are simply becoming equals. Except there are the final words of the poem: isn't that a little menacing, 'just one step behind you', where 'just' suggests he's all but caught up? And there's the end of the first stanza: 'you, out in front, unsure of your footing/on the damp stones, and me behind counting/each of your steps through our cargo of glass'. Literal, again, this description, but the figurative is close to the surface, insisted on in fact or why else have both 'you, out in front' and 'me behind ...'? We see the 'footing' they're on, the father unsteady, the son confident (trusting?) enough not to look at his own feet but to watch his father's instead, to keep the rhythm of their progress.

It's a truism in writing, especially poetry, that we should 'show not tell'. It's not just a question of respecting the reader's intelligence, leaving him or her some work to do, but also of letting the poem say what it needs to, even if we're not always altogether sure what that is. Or at least I hope it's a truism. Poem as exploration or act of discovery rather than opportunity to merely versify what we already know, usually what anybody knows, that war is bad or lost-love sad, some rather abstract theme left unparticularised and dealt with in conventional terms. Beginning poets, or poets of a certain age, feel they should write this way, usually in rhyme: if they were comics, they'd reach for the custard pies or 'I say I say I say'. Armitage, as you may know, has a poem called 'I Say I Say I Say' and it does indeed rhyme; a response, he said at a reading, to stand-up being dubbed the new rock'n'roll and poetry taking over as the new stand-up. (It's true some poetry readings are a sort of stand-up.) 'I say I say I say' is about suicide. Which we might feel is the poetry equivalent of Bob Monkhouse's 'You all laughed when I said I was going to be a comedian. You're not laughing now.'

Where I'm heading is this: though certainly like Keats we distrust poems that have a palpable design on us, we're generally equally suspicious of poems that clearly have no design at all. A poem is, or can be, made as well as discovered. 'Greenhouse' has not been content simply to detail the literal and then hope that it somehow contains the figurative; it is discreetly but artfully managed.

The opening words are one example. Another is the close of the first stanza, the reader nudged to accepting the figurative, for instance in the business about the 'footing' because it comes after the phrase 'I remember that journey'. The word 'journey' may be a likeable, idiomatic touch – just slightly hyperbolic, like when we 'take a hike', or 'get the show on the road'; but it points the symbolism behind the short distance the pair travel. Likewise that the son counts the steps through their 'cargo of glass'; Armitage is given to saying the ordinary in a mildly extraordinary way, which is entertaining for the reader, but is not merely entertainment. Without stipulating how the connotations attach to the poem overall, the poet knows we will pick them up, subliminally; for instance that 'glass is fragile' means 'they must not slip on this journey' and that the son can, literally, see through the cargo or freight they are carrying.

How else is the poem 'artful' in ways we might learn from? Firstly, it's a very user-friendly form. It looks like blank verse, but actually it's syllabic, and anyone can count syllables. Decasyllabic except for a couple of nine syllable lines (ll.19, 20), and therefore roughly pentameter, though the five stresses are distributed fairly unevenly; only occasionally is there a regular iambic, as in l.8 – 'We used the old sash windows from the house' – so the verse is disciplined but easy to keep idiomatic, natural-sounding. Similarly the piece is broken into two 13 line blocks, which gives balance, each half with its separate but related content, though it does not seem contrived. Moreover, the lines are either units of sense or else break in such a way as to emphasise the sense: 'kicked the door/out ...' for instance, or '...

your footing/on the damp stones'. The syllabics themselves seem uncontrived in their effects: that third line for instance is balanced too, but isn't obvious about it:

    the soffits lagged with a fur of cobwebs

where the two halves of the line are rhythmically identical. Art is to conceal art, as Horace says; the aim is to seem like the actor who's so good you think they're typecast. Look again at this line, for example, the least poetical in terms of diction, because the words are far from being poetry clichés, yet it's pure poetry. Having the right, rather specialised, word 'soffits' means it's concise; 'lagged with' again is from the opposite end of the 'poetical' register – we normally lag pipes – but is visually (and tactilely) accurate; as is 'fur of cobwebs', a metaphor that seems commonplace, so much a part of the narrator's voice we hardly notice it. Apart from the rhythm, what else holds the line together? Again, it's something undemonstrative, the assonance of 'soff*i*ts lagged w*i*th', and the /f/ alliteration, picked up from 'fish tank' to appear in those 'soffits' and then the 'fur'. Considering only these opening lines, we see how assonance and alliteration make their unobtrusive effect (as they do throughout the poem). Interesting, for instance, that we can't tell how Armitage pronounces 'lichen': either it takes the short /i/ assonance of 'pitted with' and therefore picks up the /t∫/ in 'each'; or else the first syllable rhymes with the next word ' like' (looking forward then to the /k/ in 'tank'). The /l/s in all this go without saying, though we mightn't have noticed them in 'walls', which word in turn brings to mind the /w/ at the end of 'now'; and then there's all those sibilants.

    At this point we need to consider what we're doing in this essay. Essentially, it's a form of practical criticism, common among teachers of creative writing; a sort of layman's stylistics, I suppose. Where it differs from other critical approaches is that it tends to go nowhere. Others use the poem as a vehicle to explore ideas or to prove a thesis; we get our heads under the bonnet or strip it down entirely and reassemble it but, speaking for myself, never learn to drive. All we need to know is how it works, so that we can make our own. In plainer terms, our job is to deal with poems as fellow practitioners, not as academics. We're interested in how the text does what it does, the nuts and bolts of it: this involves identifying poetic devices and procedures; but instead of working forwards from the text, if we move at all it's backwards, trying to discover not what the poet has achieved but why. That is, we aim to bring to ground the impulse behind the writing.

Of course this is impossible; even the poet couldn't be expected to manage it. And it may seem impertinent even to try. Well, we don't care. Though the writer tends to be (or I know Armitage feels the writer should be) courteous to the reader, s/he is quite happy to take liberties with other writers. You admire, love sometimes, another poet's work; you respect and maybe are humbled by it; but that doesn't stop you having a really good rummage. All writers do this, and because it's devices and procedures they're after, obviously you can't call it plagiarism: though you might like to compare the end of Part IV of Cowper's 'Task' with Coleridge's 'Frost at Midnight', the passage that begins: 'Therefore all seasons shall be sweet to thee'; that's effectively sampling, or, as we might call it, postmodernism. Consciously or otherwise, poets are by nature light-fingered. Even Armitage. There are allusions in his work: in the poem 'To Poverty' for instance he asks 'How have you hurt me, let me count the ways', recasting Barrett-Browning's crowd-pleaser 'How do I love thee ...'. Armitage intends us to recognise the borrowing (the original now so famous there's a key-ring, 'How do I love thee, let me count your money'). He means us to read his poem in the light of Barrett-Browning's, on which his own line is an oblique commentary. But to return to 'Greenhouse', there's a less obvious (perhaps unconscious) borrowing from a poet he happened to be reading at the time, Stanley Cook. I believe when Armitage wrote 'our cargo of glass', he was – or his poem was – thinking of Cook's line (in 'Canal') where a narrow boat sinks under its 'cargo of water'[1].

However Armitage's phrase came into being, it fits the poem, and that, in a sense, is all there is to it– for his and our purposes. Like that 'typecast' actor I mentioned a moment ago, our job is as it were to play the text, not the implications of the text. But that doesn't mean we have to be blind to those implications. Let's consider the poem again, ll. 4 to 7:

> I burst in the other day; kicked the door
> out of its warped frame, stood in the green light
> among nine years of unnatural growth
> and thought back to the morning we built it.

We respond to the contrast between energy and stillness, from bursting in to standing lost in thought; and we register the fresh use of that phrase (bordering on cliché): 'I burst in'. It seems new, here, because more usually it involves bursting in on people, a gathering, not an empty space. Then there is the wit of 'among nine years of unnatural growth': as if he is standing among time, as well as what has happened in that time, the 'unnatural growth'. And that's also interesting, that he notices what is true, but never put in those terms, about a greenhouse; and it reminds me that Armitage once quoted John Ashbery, that a poem should have at least two interesting things in every line. My point is that the poet has taken the trouble to make the writing 'interesting', and any implications a reader might infer – so long as they are not at odds with the tenor of the piece overall – must take their chance. The impulse behind the writing in this passage, I'd guess, is just that: to interest the poet (and the reader). The poem nevertheless has its own agenda, and the poet must also have been aware of it, at some level. Noting that the frame is 'warped', then that the growth is 'unnatural', can't have been accidental, or at any rate not without meaning. Dr Freud might come in with his big boots, diagnosing something sinister, and he'd be wrong (or else the poem would be more explicit elsewhere): the image is a cool appraisal, I think, of adolescence, or rather those accelerating years of childhood that end in the warped perspectives of adolescence, when we see everything only in the ('green' = naive) light of our own limited and often rather feverish experience.

Or else, in any case, you may feel these lines are merely an 'interesting' and quite literal description of what happened, which of course they are. Nevertheless, they deepen the exploration of the poem's main theme; and it is probably this theme that made the poem want to come into being, or this stanza of the poem at least. We'll return to this – what I call the 'impulse behind the writing' – shortly. As it is, we see that, after so much richness, the poet knows to deliver a plainer line at this point, 'and thought back to the morning we built it'. For Armitage that is simply a matter of technique: it calms the piece and provides a transition to the next section – 'We used the old sash windows…' – which will take us down to the point where they begin constructing the greenhouse proper. The first stanza closes on the 'cargo of glass', and the narrator opens a new stanza with the greenhouse finished and in use.

> Some nights I'd watch from my bedroom window
> as you arrived home late from a concert,
> and leaving the headlights on to guide you
> waded into the black of the garden.
> I'd wait, straining for the sound of the hasp
> or guess your distance by the sparkle
> of a cuff link. When you disturbed them
> the seeds of rose-bay willow-herbs lifted
> like air bubbles into the beam of light …

We notice the concision of the detail; the third line here, for instance, where the 'headlights' imply the car he doesn't waste space mentioning. And again, there's what Armitage is so good at: finding the absolutely ordinary specific word, in this instance, 'hasp'. There's the arresting line-break, 'sparkle/of a cuff link' and how we almost hear the echo of 'sparkle' in 'cuff link', though what we immediately respond to is the choice of this detail, and the way it allows our imagination to picture the rest of the scene. The syntax of the next sentence is another example of unshowy technical poise. Putting the subordinate clause first does no violence to the idiom, though it is unusual, and the reason is clearly to mimic the sequence of events as deduced by the onlooker: 'When you disturbed them/the seeds of rose-bay willow-herbs …'. This way round, we're as much in the dark to start with as the narrator until we see what it is has been disturbed, lifting into the light.

Now we come to something unprovable, contentious to say the least, and ultimately anyway irrelevant. That is, we come to consider the impulse behind the main extended image of the second stanza. I suspect most writers do this, though they may not realise it, this sourcing of the 'impulse behind' the poem or features in the poem. It is asking why the poem came to do what it does, and though this must involve the what and how of it – a run of alliteration, for instance and its effect on the reader – we're not much interested in that effect.

The key words in the opening of the second half of the poem seem to me 'wade into' and those 'seeds' rising 'like air-bubbles'. Art conceals art here because, until the 'air bubbles', the expression of the father wading in is merely a dead metaphor, appropriate in the situation because it suggests a sort of determined recklessness, and also the way that your walk does change, walking into pitch black, not unlike walking into water. The simile of the 'air-bubbles' is accurate too; that is, we feel that's just what the seeds must look like as they rise and are picked out by the headlights. Together, though, 'wade' and 'air-bubbles' put the whole scene underwater, and make the father's trip to the greenhouse almost like heroism. Well, of course it doesn't do that; he's only gone to get some tomatoes after all. But it does show that the son sees him as a bit of a hero. There's something else too, though, isn't there? Something figurative about the blackness of the garden and the father there in that (submerged) greenhouse.

A theory could be put forward, I expect, to make sense of it; but I want to go back instead to them building the greenhouse from their 'cargo of glass'; and how the poet has built this (if he did), from another poem, from Stanley Cook's image of the 'cargo of water'. It's extremely tenuous to suppose the greenhouse and the father in the greenhouse are underwater because the son's imagination was prompted in this way, and even if Cook's 'cargo of water' is behind the second stanza, it makes no useful difference to the finished poem. But it is useful to us, as writers. Or this particular explanation is useful to me: you may not – probably don't – agree with it; but it satisfies my reading of the poem. We all approach this differently, but since we have only ourselves – our own writing – to answer to, our suppositions don't have to work for anyone else. This kind of 'prompting', or deep intertextuality, must occur often, and perhaps goes unregarded even by the writer. It is a corollary of what seems to happen in any 'organic' writing. Keats remarks for example that 'things which [I] do half at Random are afterwards confirmed by my judgement in a dozen features of Propriety' [Letter to Haydon, 11 May 1817]. 'Half at Random': it's a marvellously liberating phrase; though we notice also the subsequent appeal to 'judgement' and the test of 'Propriety': the detail or image must pull its weight in the poem, and must sit well with, if not amplify, the other detail. It brings to mind Keats's friend Richard Woodhouse, who noted that Keats 'has not been aware of the beauty of some thought or expression until after he has composed & written it down—It has then struck him with astonishment—& seemed rather the production of another person than his own—He has wondered how he came to hit upon it.' [The Keats Circle, 129; quoted Ricks, *Keats and Embarrassment* 1990: 73]

It is easy to overstress the principle of organicism in composition; and though a common failing in student work is that it isn't 'organic' enough (that the writer has been too conscious throughout, rather than allowing the poem to develop 'as naturally as the leaves to the tree'), it's equally true that a poem can lack organisation. Sometimes it's just that the writer goes under the spell of the sound of the words, and loses sight of the sense. Occasionally this has to do with using a 'poetical' diction, words you'd never use in a letter or conversation. The afternoon's rarely 'dank' for instance, except in poems. The point about this – using 'a myriad' instead of 'lots' – is not so much that it stinks of 'poetry' (when art is to conceal art), but that it is a borrowed diction. It's almost always better to use our own, or one at least that sounds like a person, not a nineteenth century anthology. Look at the diction in 'Greenhouse' for instance.

On the other hand, poems aren't merely letters or conversation (though some are written as letters, or pretend to be conversation). 'Greenhouse', as we've seen, tends actually to disguise its 'poetry', though there are plenty of poetical devices, such as alliteration, assonance, simile, metaphor and so on. It's true that this is partly a matter of diction, or rather the voice, the way the poem seems naturally to talk rather than at the reader. But it's also to do with the poem's form, which is metrically relaxed and avoids end-rhyme, so that, laid out as prose, you might not guess its original shape.

'Poem'

It's fair to suppose there was, once the poem got underway, a slight controlling pressure of form in 'Greenhouse', each line roughly the same length and so partly dictating (consciously or otherwise) the choice of phrasing to best suit the line breaks. But form can have a much greater say in how a poem gets written, as this final example shows. Far from disguising its poetry, it's actually called 'Poem':

> And if it snowed, and snow lay on the drive
> he took a spade and tossed it to one side.
> And always tucked his daughter up at night.
> And slippered her the one time that she lied.
>
> And every week he tipped up half his wage.
> And what he didn't spend each week he saved.
> And praised his wife for every meal she made.
> And once, for laughing, punched her in the face.
>
> And for his mum he hired a private nurse.
> And every Sunday taxied her to church.
> And he blubbed when she went from bad to worse.
> And twice he lifted ten quid from her purse.
>
> Here's how they rated him when they looked back:
> sometimes he did this, sometimes he did that.

Clearly, this is highly organised. Apart from the opening and closing couplets, every line is end-stopped, and each begins with 'And'. Apart from the closing couplet, every line is regular iambic pentameter:

> And íf| it snówed| and snów| lay ón| the dríve ...

There are three quatrains, or four-line stanzas, and a final couplet; which suggests a sonnet, though customised: it is not one of the given rhyme schemes and does not divide in sense after the eighth (or tenth) line. Instead of interleaved (abab) or closed-quatrain (abba) full-rhyme, in fact, we have mono- rhymed quatrains (aaaa). Stanza three has three full-rhymes – 'nurse', 'worse', 'purse' – but by this stage the reader is accustomed to hearing only the assonance ('church', 'worse'), the vowel-rhyme which largely governs the other stanzas. Full-rhyme does occur on lines 1 and 3 ('side', 'lied'), but full- rhymed quatrains throughout might have been too rich. For the same reason, the poem avoids simile and metaphor and though there is alliteration and also other internal assonance, this is generally more sparing than in 'Greenhouse' (which has no end-rhyme or regular metre). There is one other element of patterning, and this is in sense or content: each stanza details three 'positive' examples of the man's behaviour against one 'negative' line. The ratio three-to-one seems to favour the positive, though the negative examples, being what they are, and given last in each stanza, more than balance out: stanza two, for instance: half the wage; prudence with money; praising the cooking, these are overturned by the single instance of violence.

This line, 'And once, for laughing, punched her in the face', shows the poem's concision, giving shorthand ('for laughing') from which the reader fills out the story. Though called 'Poem', what we have is a sort of biography, in fact – the laconic penultimate line 'when they looked back' lets us know the man has died. The indifference of the ending, delivered in distributed metre (spoken rhythms, not iambics), asks us to consider how our view differs from the way 'they' rate the man. I think this is one reason Armitage has chosen the title he has, very much to point the relationship the poet (and reader) has with the character who 'exists' only in the textworld, a man who in a sense is merely a creation of the 'Poem'; and how in the end a person's life may mean just as little to his acquaintances; also, which attaches to Keats's notion of writing 'half at Random', how un-patterned, undesigned a life is: 'sometimes he did this, sometimes he did that'.

Although the poem by contrast is highly patterned and insists on its status as text, 'Poem' is far from artificial in diction or terms of reference. We notice the idiomatic phrases: ' tipped up half his wage'; 'taxied her to church; 'lifted ten quid from her purse'. Part of the pleasure of the poem is the skill with which Armitage accommodates the everyday idiom and perspective into its form. What we might learn from it is that it is a very deliberate performance; the poem's structure and patterning may have suggested themselves as composition got underway, but quite early on Armitage must have decided to organise his material this way: and, crucially, to allow some of the material itself to be suggested by the form. The poem may arrive organically, but there is much more input, so to speak, from formal pressure, and this has led to an appreciably smaller contract between texture of language and imagery in composition of the piece.

NOTE
[1] Stanley Cook, *Woods Beyond A Cornfield: Collected Poems* (Smith/Doorstop, 1995), p.11.

REFERENCES
'Greenhouse' and 'It Ain't What You Do, It's What It Does To You' are from *Zoom!* (Bloodaxe, 1989). 'Poem' is from *Kid* (Faber, 1992). All three are on *Zoom! and Other Poems* (Smith/Doorstop audio-cassette, 1991).

Living Dolls and Broken Machines: Caricatural Effects in Ian McMillan, Carol Ann Duffy and Geoff Hattersley

Ian Gregson

Ian McMillan

Ian McMillan – like a number of other British poets who emerged in the early 80's, poets such as John Ash and Peter Didsbury – is a self-conscious postmodernist. In McMillan's case this is linked to his most important quality as a poet which is that he is very funny. His poem 'Against Realism', for example, makes a postmodernist point about the difference between the 'real world' and what happens to it in poems, however 'realistic', but it does so with the combination of faithfully rendered colloquial speech and surreal comedy that make his poems such fun to read:

> At the poetry workshop
> the woman holds up a plum.
>
> 'Can I read this poem about a plum?'
> she says.
>
> 'That is a very well written poem
> about a plum,' I say.
>
> 'It is a plum!'
> someone shouts.
>
> 'It is certainly very fine writing.'
> I reply, wittily.

However, McMillan is most interesting when he combines his postmodern comedy with his own form of political satire. This is a unique combination but it can be best understood in the context of forms of caricatural art whose impact in the postwar period has been too little studied. So some of the components of recent texts which have been described as 'postmodernist' can be more specifically related to the much older tradition of caricature which influenced both visual and literary artists including Swift and Dickens, Hogarth and Daumier. The impact of this inheritance in the past forty years has been most obvious in satirical writings. Its key images depict the human as reduced to the status of an object, an animal or a machine, or the human body as dismembered to represent the fragmentation of the human spirit.

These caricatural images intersect with postmodern anxieties about the self because they question the boundaries of the human. They have proven to be especially useful to writers concerned to satirise the impact of capitalism on human identity, the impact of what Michele Hannoosh – discussing the cartoons of Jean Grandville – calls 'the fragmentation, commodification, and dehumanization of experience in capitalist culture'[1]. I'll be tracing the source of caricatural techniques in the poems of Ian McMillan and Geoff Hattersley to their shared concerns in this thematic area and more specifically to their concerns with the human consequences of post-industrial economic decline in south Yorkshire. Their most powerful work depicts characters who have been radically dehumanised by this economic experience and it draws upon caricatural imagery to evoke this dehumanisation as a form of dismemberment or exhaustion of the self. Similarly, Carol Ann Duffy repeatedly refers to the caricatural idea of dummies and puppets in order to explore issues related to gender domination and subordination.

However, what is happening in these poets can only be thoroughly understood in the context of the widespread deployment of caricatural themes and effects in other writers and in recent culture generally. A similar outlook is expressed in more populist forms, for example, in some of the animated cartoons and their like that have appeared on television in the past thirty years. These would include Terry Gilliam's animations for *Monty Python*, the satirical puppets used in *Spitting Image*, and the angrier moments in *The Simpsons* and *South Park*. All of these arise out of a caricatural sensibility with its tendency to savage misanthropy, its distaste for the human body and its profound mistrust of mainstream culture and those in authority.

Another important overlap between postmodernism and caricature is in how both subvert realism and its assumptions. This partly accounts for why postmodernist authors have drawn upon caricatural effects which can mock realist conventions – 'fully-rounded' characters, linear plotting etc – with confrontational comedy. The most crucial point here is that post modernist authors have questioned the humanist assumptions behind realism – how 'fully-roundedness' takes for granted that human personality is complex, coherent, substantial and capable of endless development. This overlap is relevant to how some 'magic realist' characterisation is caricatural in its deliberate confusing of the human with animals and things and its deliberate refusal to bestow vividly 'human' uniqueness on its characters (the way for example Garcia Marquez's *One Hundred Years of Solitude* contains seventeen characters dismissively called Aureliano). It is for this reason that Charles Dickens, one of the key authors in the caricatural tradition, could be described as 'magic realist' *avant la lettre*. It is for this reason, too, that caricatural effects and 'surreal' ones are often indistinguishable from each other.

McMillan is most clearly postmodernist in his favourite poetic strategy which involves mingling diverse genres and registers to produce a comic effect and to destabilise textual expectations. 'Propp's Last Case'[2] has an epigraph that claims to be from an unpublished critical work by McMillan himself, entitled *Trends in 't Yorkshire Novel*

> Occasionally, during the late 50's and early 60's, the dominant position of the realist Yorkshire novel was challenged by a number of American-influenced works known as the hardboiled school of Yorkshire prose.

To say that what follows is a brief description of a sexual encounter that seems unsure whether it is being written by John Braine or Raymond Chandler, however, would be to underestimate its instability. 'It was unthinkable midnight or Autumn/ in a blackish Barnsley of the mind' comically turns the reliable setting of a 50's novel into something questionable and subjective, or textual – a place out of a novel and therefore fictive (however realistic the novel). But the disagreement, as it were, between 'unthinkable' and 'mind' further suggests that this novelistic Barnsley is being defamiliarised by an unprecedented experience, or another text. The realist novel is in this way interrogated by conventions unfamiliar to it – first of all by those of the detective story which characteristically start with the central figure 'in the dark'. This is partly why Barnsley is 'blackish' and it is 'unthinkable midnight'. But then they are questioned much further by the conventions of postmodernist poems – 'midnight or Autumn' need not be alternatives, but presented as such playfully refer to the fictive activity of defining chronology, and this is made more explicit later when the two are referred to as 'interchangeable'. Before this, however, a further generic doubt is introduced with a reference to radio plays, so that – given the possibility that this is a narrative whose only medium is sound – the midnight or Autumn alternative acquires a new lease of witty irrelevance. But then this too is subverted when the joke about the arbitrariness of fictive settings turns into a joke about the arbitrariness of fictive naming; the speaker thinks that midnight or Autumn might refer to lingerie but they turn out to refer to dogs which chase him until he gasps 'like they gasp/ just before they die/ on radio plays'.

This kind of playfulness is McMillan's most conspicuous characteristic but repeatedly his poems have a sombre undertow arising partly from a sense that the pervasiveness of the fictive may be connected with a sense of loss or incapacity rather than increased potential. It is here, in particular, that his version of postmodernism most intersects with caricature because it is linked to how McMillan's imagery hints, surprisingly often, at a reification or mutilation of the human.

This can be better understood by reference to the ways that caricatural effects are drawn upon by the American novelist Joseph Heller whose satirical focus is repeatedly on institutions (the military-industrial complex, corporate business, the government in Washington) which have been shaped by the devotion to money. The depiction of the consequent impact of commodification on every area of human experience underlies Heller's most brilliant writing. It is this idea that lies behind Heller's obsessive habit of depicting his characters as turned into things or broken into pieces. The 'soldier in white' in *Catch-22* is the most extreme example of this, 'encased from head to toe in plaster and gauze' (16) reduced to the 'frayed black hole over his mouth' and 'filed next to the Texan' (17).

However, *Catch-22* does not make these points simply as an 'anti-war' book. Heller has said that he regards it as 'essentially a peacetime book'[4] and what it does above all is to depict the madness of war in order to insist on the systemic craziness of capitalism. *Catch-22* reveals how the political system displays itself more clearly *in extremis*, how war brings its mechanisms to the surface. This also provides justification for Heller's confrontationally simplistic method in the novel, how he represents the army as an enterprise and a bureaucracy whose business is to promote death.

Caricatural imagery similar to that of *Catch-22* is present in other late twentieth century texts. What this represents is a radical reappraisal of human identity itself in this period: it is linked to that characteristically postmodern interrogation of the wholeness and uniqueness of the self. Heller is closest to McMillan, Duffy and Hattersley at the point where this interrogation takes a political form, at the point where its presentation of 'character' as radically reduced is made for satirical ends. In 'The er Barnsley Seascapes'[5] McMillan presents the post-industrial landscape as a sort of surreal cartoon. British Coal has sold the houses and

> made us live
> in heads.
>
> great big
> severed heads.
>
> Rows of heads
> overlooking the sea.
>
> Sometimes I stand
> in the eyes
>
> and I cry.
> Then I burn
>
> the tears.
> Cheaper than coal. (84)

The reference to severed heads makes a similar point to the last line of McMillan's 'The Tennis Ball Factory Poems': 'We have lost our bastard hands' (*Selected*, 54). The imagery of shattered body parts represents the shattering of the self – its coherence has been broken by the purposelessness imposed on it. It is also linked to the imagery of 'Just the Facts, Just the' where the speaker's daughter is said to be 'jerking'

> about on the settee, bright red,
> making little cardboard cries.
>
> cardboard cries? Pull together yourself.
> (*Selected*, 83)

The collocation of cardboard and cries is made even more disturbing here by the way it follows the syntactical ambiguity surrounding 'bright red' which makes it able to apply both to the child and the settee. This is all from the father's perspective and registers his shock at finding his daughter's behaviour so alien that she comes to resemble an object – a shock which is reflected in his recoil, in the next lines, from his own phrase, then in his jumbled word-order and finally in his lapse into silence.

In 'The er Barnsley Seascapes' the idea of alienness is more clearly political and therefore more clearly related to notions of alienation. As a result, this poem's depiction of things becoming (fragmentarily) human, and the human becoming a thing is satirically directed at how pit closures have made men unable, as it were, to pull together themselves. The language of the poem is similarly troubled, its repeated faltering into 'er', especially in the titles of individual sections ('Little Houghton seascape er like') suggesting its colloquial incapacity to pull together itself into full articulacy. Part of the point here is regional because, as McMillan has said, South Yorkshiremen 'don't talk very much': 'Don't ask me why that is, it could be all those years of bad industrial news, all those years of pits shutting and steelworks locking their gates'[6]. This means that 'South Yorkshire minimalists' sometimes run out of words altogether and resort to 'cries and moans' especially 'Eeee'. That moan replaces speech altogether. By contrast 'er' is a faltering connective, as also is 'like' which can be used punningly to suggest an aborted simile. The minimalism of this particular poem, then, arises from a linguistic fragmentariness linked to the poem's depiction of a whole landscape broken into pieces.

This linguistic self-consciousness is of a piece with the textual self-consciousness and self-reflexivity which characterises McMillan's work as a whole and which most identifies him as a postmodernist. However, the specifically regional element that lies behind it draws attention to McMillan's simultaneous resistance to much of what postmodernism represents culturally and politically. This personal ambiguity is also evident in 'South Yorkshire Minimalism' where he identifies himself as a South Yorkshireman but also an 'unusual' one because he is a media personality who talks for a living. This also complicates the authorial viewpoint that lies behind 'The er Barnsley Seascapes'. On the one hand this is a scathing political poem linked to the realist elements in his work as a whole. His poems after all are solidly grounded in the territory of social realism – set mostly in Yorkshire, they refer to mines and factories and to a landscape where the industrial and rural meet; their rhythms and assonances are vividly linked to the poet's own broad accent, and they occasionally employ dialect. On the other hand, however 'The er Barnsley Seascapes' draws upon a postmodern mingling of registers and textual references which make it complicit with the postindustrial culture it satirises. It is this culture which is associated with educated outsiders who try to record the 'dying tradition' of 'er Barnsley' on their 'Japanese tape recorders' and who write a learned paper about it that combines an academic register with surreal flights of fantasy.

This ambiguity in McMillan's position is fascinating because it suggests that being politically compromised by postmodernism is inescapable. Like the other South Yorkshire celebrities he mentions in 'South Yorkshire Minimalism' – Brian Glover, Michael Parkinson, Dickie Bird – McMillan depends upon his South Yorkshire roots for his subject matter, but like them, too, he has to have grown away from those roots in order to be able to articulate what they mean. Where genuine South Yorkshireman merely say 'Eeee', McMillan writes poems and broadcasts on radio and T.V. This makes him a conspicuous beneficiary of the culture which has replaced the heavy industry whose loss is ambiguously grieved over in 'The er Barnsley

Seascapes', where the spectacle of loss is poetically enjoyed as much as it is suffered.

What is important in this is that the loss of 'genuineness' this involves is representative of a loss of such genuineness in everyone, a loss of 'integrity' in both senses and its replacement by complex postmodern compromise. It is partly this which makes postmodern humanity seem caricatural in comparison with its realist and Romantic predecessors where social surface concealed a unique soul. One key image in the caricatural tradition, by contrast, is of the human compromised by the inhuman, the human infiltrated or edged with the animal, the object or the machine, so that its boundaries are called into question.

Carol Ann Duffy

This is also a key effect in Carol Ann Duffy's 'Small Female Skull'[6] where the speaker holds her own severed head disorientingly in her own hands. Observed like this it is so thoroughly defamiliarised that it resembles an ocarina and is said to have the weight of 'a deck of cards, a slim volume of verse'. This is shocking because it associates what we now take to be the centre of our being with mere things. It seems appropriate, then, that she thinks that 'Downstairs they will think I have lost my mind' because the mind is worryingly equated with the skull, with what is only physical and will definitely die, and is therefore not the core of self that might previously have been regarded as potentially transcendent and immortal.

However, the key line that links this poem to Duffy's central concerns is the one that refers to her taking the skull 'to the mirror to ask for a gottle of geer'. This mimicking of the speech of ventriloquists and their implied failure to transpose that speech entirely convincingly into the mouths of their dummies indicates that 'Small Female Skull' turns the detached skull into a poetic mouthpiece that can define (though with explicit falteringness) what the speaker's self is and how it is constituted out of memories whose traces it bears, as in 'the scar where I fell for sheer love/ down treacherous stairs'. The crucial idea here is that this distorted voice works as an analogy for poetic 'voices', especially in dramatic monologue which is one of Duffy's favourite idioms. In relating this to ventriloquy she is relating it to a recurrent motif of the caricatural tradition in which the image of dolls and dummies is used to satirise the total domination by one country, or by one political figure, of another which is reduced to its 'puppet'. This was a self-reflexive premise in *Spitting Image* whose victims were all transformed into more or less grotesque dummies and voiced by impressionists. Once this premise was established it was a small step, for example, to suggest that Ronald Reagan was literally brainless and had to have his brain inserted each morning by aides. A similar idea is at work in Gerald Scarfe's 'Nixon is Right Behind You' where Henry Kissinger is depicted as merely a sort of mask with Nixon crouching darkly behind it.

Duffy's use of the dummy motif is linked directly to her politics which are anti-establishment and feminist. Her poems are driven by the desire to give a voice to those who are habitually spoken *for*, and often explore how masculinist ways of seeing determine how women are regarded, even by themselves, and how language determines the experiences it is supposed merely to describe – how representation makes dummies of us all. So in 'Standing Female Nude' (20-1) the overlapping of different discourses reveals how the artist's model's body is transformed as her own familiar way of thinking about it is quickly reoriented in painterly terms – 'Belly nipple arse in the window light'. The use of dramatic monologue is all the more significant here because it suggests the extent to which she is made to rethink herself from the point of view of a masculine aesthetic.

This concern with the caricatural effect of the male gaze hints at how the dummy motif in Duffy is linked to the image of dolls which recurs in feminist fictions. The reifying and, occasionally, mechanising of the human that is implied in the doll image clearly links it to those concerns in the caricatural tradition. An especially striking version of this image echoes throughout Joyce Carol Oates' recent novel *Blonde*[8]. This is a fictionalised biography of Marilyn Monroe who is presented, like Duffy's model, as reduced by the male gaze to a metonymic embodiment of the female, reduced – as 'Sugar Kane', who is a 'sex cartoon', in *Some Like It Hot* – to 'the female buttocks, breasts', and to a 'ukulele … pursued by male saxophones' (613).

She is a 'foam-rubber sex doll' (444), a 'blond mannequin' (616). Being a star in the masculinist cinema of her time commodifies Monroe: she is a 'cash cow' (563) whose own identity gets lost in the fantasised travesties of her which are her screen image:

> She was 'Marilyn' – no, she was 'Angela' – she was Norma Jean playing 'Marilyn' playing 'Angela' – like a Russian doll in which smaller dolls are contained by the largest doll   (256)

Carol Ann Duffy draws upon the resources of dramatic monologue to allow the dummy to speak back and so resist its reification and reassert its personhood. In 'The Dummy' this happens literally:

> Why do you
> keep me in that black box? I can ask questions, too,
> you know. I can see that worries you. Tough.   (36)

This indicates how a person's language can be colonised and works analogously in this respect to the self-reflexive element in most of Duffy's dramatic monologues. The political point, above all, is that much of the language we speak infiltrates us from outside. This self-reflexiveness also asks to what extent the self is composed of the language that it speaks, and, combined with Duffy's satire against patriarchal structures, it struggles against the masculine values that the language always already expresses.

In suggesting that masculine attitudes lead to caricatural distortiveness Duffy has a surprising precursor in post-war poetry in Ted Hughes who increasingly in middle and later life became a sort of eco-feminist. His book *Shakespeare and the Goddess of Complete Being*[9] expresses this ideology most thoroughly and reveals why the key idea in Hughes's work from *Wodwo*[10] onwards is that the rise of Protestantism represents a systemic rejection of the feminine which inflicts dire consequences on Western culture. He sees this, mythically, as involving the rejection of the figure of the Goddess – a sort of transcendent feminine principle, as represented by Venus in Shakespeare's 'Venus and Adonis' – and the simultaneous move towards the masculine rationalism that lies behind Protestantism and capitalism. The crucial idea behind *Crow*[11] is that this has diminished human potential so far that humanity has reduced itself to a monstrous caricature. When Crow runs from the water-spirit he is mutilated, he is 'One-legged, gutless and brainless, the rag of himself' (43), when he attacks his mother with technology his head falls off 'like a leaf' (70). Similarly, 'A Bedtime Story' (71-2) describes a man who is 'intermittent', has 'only half a face', his hands are 'funny hooves', 'Half his head was jellyfish'. 'A Grin' (29), 'In Laughter' (48-9) and 'The Smile' (62-3) all explore the idea of the cruel comedy that arises from caricature, that derives entertainment from the spectacle of humiliating diminishment and disintegration.

The emphasis of both the Shakespeare book and Hughes' later poetry is to heal the violent divisiveness that arises from what he calls the 'peculiar division of the sexes' and their 'peculiar conflict'. But it is in *Crow* that Hughes diagnoses the sickness and it is in that volume that the words 'division', 'conflict' and maybe, above all, 'peculiar' seem most relevant. *Crow* is a brilliant examination of the damage caused by the attempts of masculinity to define itself against, and establish its independence from femininity. The anthropomorphic element in the early animal poems is implicit: by contrast *Crow* draws upon the long tradition of caricature which satirises human shortcomings by depicting human/animal hybrids – in order to dwell on male incorrigibleness and destructiveness. This is partly explained by the fact that the poems were written, at Leonard Baskin's invitation, to accompany that American artist's drawings. But throughout *Crow*, as everywhere else in this tradition, the stress is on a form of reduction which has the stark energy of single-mindedness. There is crucially a sense of something missing, of the confrontational lack of the richness and complexity which humanism associates with the self – but the sense, also, that this very lack produces, paradoxically, a larger than life impact.

Carol Ann Duffy's feminism is very different from Hughes' and has none of his Gravesian/ Jungian mysticism which eventually, as I point out in my book *The Male Image*[12], proves very damaging to him. Like him, however, she is preoccupied with the distortions of the self caused by sexist attitudes and it is this which draws her to the use of caricatural effects. More unusually and more impressively, however, she is aware of how much patriarchy also caricatures men – how much its imperatives make masculinity predictable and one-dimensional. It is largely this that makes her 'Psychopath' (43-6) the subtle poem that it is, and makes it work so hard to evoke the sense of an actual man and actual events. It painstakingly establishes a 50's setting and characterises its speaker as a working-class figure operating in a series of working-class milieux which are evoked with careful realist notation – the fairground, in particular, with its candyfloss, its goldfish, its coconuts and its Tunnel of Love.

All of this has an especially powerful impact because it is placed in dialogue with the poem's postmodernist elements which draw attention to how much the psychopath's image is distorted. The presence, so strongly hinted at, of the poet's voice in 'Psychopath' is a way of owning up to the extent to which the 'psychopath' is being caricatured, especially because the reader's sense of the implied author as a didactic feminist arouses an acute feeling that the psychopathic voice speaks entirely against the grain of her beliefs. The imagery of the poem literally reflects this suspicion in its recurrent dwelling on the psychopath's 'image' – 'I run my metal comb through the D.A. and pose/ my reflection between dummies in the window at Burton's'. The shifts that are involved as the reader watches the speaker watching himself are important because they draw attention to the question of how what is seen is interpreted. The middle section starts with an indication that the ability to reflect (and therefore to represent) is defeated by the nature of the man himself, and perhaps by his language – 'My breath wipes me from the looking-glass'. In a sense this is the psychopath answering the poet back – rebuking her for speaking through him like a ventriloquist. The reference to 'dummies' in the second line is not an accident, then, because it draws attention to the extent to which the psychopath is a mere simulacrum.

Duffy's fascination with dummies and ventriloquy is part of her key political concern with the patriarchal dynamics of domination and subordination. Here again postmodernism and caricature intersect because this is a form of politics which is focused on issues of representation so that caricatural effects are called upon self-reflexively to indicate textual – and, by analogy, political – distortiveness.

A less political version of this motivates Ian McMillan's 'Ted Hughes Is Elvis Presley' (*Donkey*, 19-21) where the comic combining of the two eponymous figures drains them both of any individual reality. Both of them are present only in the cartoon versions of them which are their public 'images'. It is only at this level that they can even remotely be joined together though this remoteness achieves the sense of incongruity on which the poem's comedy depends. Their only shared characteristic is physical size and even here Hughes' formidable physique is only travestied when equated with Elvis' obesity. When 'Elvis' declares himself to have been 'too, too big' (19), however, it is clear that the word is being used to refer to fame and its oppressiveness and therefore to refer to the poem's exploration of the impact of celebrity on the self. The self-conscious reduction of an important issue to its half-dismissive representation by a physical characteristic is a staple idea of the caricatural tradition. It is called upon by McMillan here to characteristically ambiguous effect because it satirises postmodern 'image' construction but simultaneously celebrates it. The Hughes/ Presley hybrid enacts the postmodern flattening of aesthetic hierarchies. The satire here might be said to mock the way that the poet laureate becomes a public performer like any other, but the spectacle of Hughes as Presley lacks any satirical anger. However, it's certainly very funny:

> At my poetry readings I sneer and rock my hips.
> I stride the moors
> in a white satin jump suit
> bloated as the full moon.
> (20)

Geoff Hattersley

This interest in postmodern celebrity and hybrid identity is very alien to the outlook of Geoff Hattersley who in other ways is very close to Ian McMillan, especially in their shared preoccupation with the industrial decline of South Yorkshire. By contrast with the energetic surface of 'Ted Hughes Is Elvis Presley' the surfaces of Hattersley's poems are deadpan and minimal – he is himself a genuine South Yorkshire minimalist, and presents himself as almost seamlessly a part of his working-class environment. It is mostly out of this deadpan minimalism that Hattersley's deployment of caricature arises because it is this that he uses to portray his South Yorkshire characters – in their response to the political times – as flattened by terminal exhaustion or transformed into faulty mechanisms.

One exception to this, which is important because it is one of Hattersley's best known poems, is 'The Cigar'[13] where he employs much more flagrant caricature in a much more straightforwardly political idiom. Here the cigar is deployed to represent American weaponry and phallic power which is equated with megalomaniac greed: an American lights the cigar with a blow-torch before 'the cartoon gapes of the other customers' and it then begins 'to expand at an alarming rate'. The use in this poem of the idea of personal consumption to represent imperialism is reminiscent of James Gillray's 1805 cartoon 'The Plum-Pudding in Danger' which depicts Napoleon and William Pitt carving up the world which is sitting like a plum-pudding on the table in front of them.

Aside from this exception, however, his poems characteristically observe people doing nothing or almost nothing, or doing something pointless or self-destructive. He has evolved a style that much of the time also seems, itself, to be doing almost nothing, especially in its choice of materials and methods of organising them. This means that his development has been away from explicit gestures such as those that occasionally damage his early small press collection *Port of Entry* (Littlewood Press, 1989). In that book 'Almost Unbelievably' declares that 'History repeats itself' and refers to diaries as 'palimpsests' – pretentious moments that are now unthinkable for Hattersley. The ending of that poem though looks forward to what he now does and says most tellingly:

> When the toast caught fire
> last night and the grill
> it was the most exciting event
> here for at least three years.

Hattersley's use, these days, of deadpan description of one action and then another may well have Frank O'Hara's 'I do this I do that' technique behind it as an ancestor. There's a similarly minimal element in terms of authorial reaction; Hattersley's tendency, though is to marginalise himself and to imply his own passiveness. This is crucially different from O'Hara's focus on himself being purposeful and talkative. The environments are similarly contrasted. O'Hara's New York is glamorous and self-important and complements the campily flagrant narcissism of his part in it. Hattersley's 'New Yorkshire' (as his two Bloodaxe blurbs have *both* labelled it) is derelict and dysfunctional, and his responses are glum and taciturn, or wryly dismissive.

The gender contrasts here are significant – the one self-consciously gay, the other flatly masculine and straight. However, the class contrasts are also important. O'Hara depicts himself in the business of being curator of the Museum of Modern Art; his outlook is leisured and aesthetic, he's preoccupied with books, films and shopping; his context is post-war American prosperity.

O'Hara's New York was a happening place: in Hattersley's South Yorkshire industrial decline ensures that things no longer happen. O'Hara's characters are artists and poets: Hattersley's are old or directionless like the one who says he's not interested in changing the world, 'it's hard enough remembering/ to change my underpants'. The most emotional moments have an air of parody ('He knows he's done wrong but wrong was done to him too') as though emotion was something people *used* to have.

The focus on tiredness and desperation can produce a throwaway effect so that his poems can seem to amount only to one shrug after another. However, an implied politics emerges insinuatingly and quizzically. The poem called 'Politics'[14] reveals why this is the most appropriate way for this to emerge. Here the current political situation is evoked metaphorically through two scenes. The first is about being at your own funeral and no-one hearing when you shout that you're alive. Feelings of frustration and powerlessness are also present in the second scene but joined here by the quizzical resignation that characterises so many Hattersley poems: two men confront each other in a power relationship which only clarifies after years pass during which 'Ice forms on the cameras/ that bring us news'. It's only after this that one gets the other to jump through a hoop in a surreal literalising of that figure of speech.

What is powerful about this aspect of Hattersley is how it evokes the *complexity* of a current politics which makes simple anger seem too crude and usually misdirected, and evokes the bafflement of the political victims about where their oppression comes from. It is in these contexts that Hattersley's surreal moments work best and where they are most joined by caricatural effects – where they suggest a radical deformation of the human, the normalising of what ought to be sadly abnormal. So alongside the Hattersley characters who seem politically (in this larger context) paralysed into inactivity, there are others who are driven by bizarre compulsions which are like distorted memories of purpose, like the builder who surrounds a woman with a fence so that only the top of her head is visible, and then greets the poet:

> 'Morning ter yer,'
> he says to me;
> he's knocking a steel post
> into my front doorstep;
> 'nearly done, nearly done'.

This builder is like a character in *Catch-22* in being terminally self-absorbed, self-destructively compulsive and so one-dimensional he is entirely inaccessible to others. Given how clear Hattersley's socialist affiliations are in his poems, the use of Marxist terms like alienation and reification are entirely appropriate to account for the political processes by which Hattersley's characters have been reduced to caricatures: this is why 'Straight' (55) is about depletion and 'God and Bananas'(54) about terminal tiredness, about being reduced to a 'brown stain'. This is character diminished to its final point; it is caricatural minimalism whittled down *beyond* the minimum.

NOTES

[1] Michele Hannoosh, *Baudelaire and Caricature* (Pennsylvania State University Press, 1992) 163

[2] Ian McMillan, *Selected Poems* (Carcanet, 1987) 76-77. Henceforth *Selected*

[3] Joseph Heller, *Catch-22* (Vintage, 1994), first published 1961

[4] Paul Krassner, 'An Impolite Interview with Joseph Heller', in *The Best of 'The Realist'* (Running Press (Philadelphia) 1984) 79

[5] Ian McMillan, *Dad, the Donkey's on Fire* (Carcanet, 1994) 82-6
Henceforth *Donkey*

[6] Ian McMillan, *I Found This Shirt* (Carcanet, 1998) 82

[7] Carol Ann Duffy, *Selected Poems* (Penguin, 1994) 109-10 All references to Duffy are to this volume

[8] Joyce Carol Oates, *Blonde* (Fourth Estate, 2000)

[9] Ted Hughes, *Shakespeare and the Goddess of Complete Being* (Faber, 1992)

[10] Ted Hughes, *Wodwo* (Faber, 1967)

[11] Ted Hughes, *Crow* (Faber, 1972)

[12] Ian Gregson, *The Male Image: Representations of Masculinity in Postwar Poetry* (Macmillan, 1999)

[13] Geoff Hattersley, *Don't Worry* (Bloodaxe, 1994) 12

[14] Geoff Hattersley, *On the Buses With Dostoevsky* (Bloodaxe, 1998) 46

Beyond the referential: rootedness and fluidity in the poetry of Gillian Clarke

Diane Davies

Gillian Clarke is widely admired both within and beyond the borders of Wales, where she has spent most of her life. Her service to poetry and motivation of others through workshops, radio programmes and readings are impressively recorded in *Trying the Line: A Volume of Tribute to Gillian Clarke*, edited by Menna Elfyn, who introduces Clarke as a poet whose 'commitment to turning listeners into writers, and passive audiences into readers is surely without rival', even describing her as 'an ambassador for Wales in the wider world'.[1] In spite of belonging to what was for most of the twentieth century called the 'Anglo-Welsh' literary tradition and often represented as deficient to Welsh-language writing in its dependence on the English language for the expression of Welsh identity and experience, Clarke appears today to be respected virtually in equal measure by the Welsh and English writing communities of Wales. Her broad popularity is easily explained: she is articulately loyal to a Welsh cultural heritage and supportive of the Welsh language without being nationalistic; she privileges her geographical origins in relation to place and community without cutting herself off from diversity and internationalism; she has opened up new ground for female and feminised experience in her writing while acknowledging the validity of the work of women silenced or restricted by traditional gender roles.

Clarke's poetry does not immediately invite deconstruction, since the boundaries of her poetic territory would appear to be clearly marked and firmly maintained. Gates do not seem to be left open through which she might lead the reader towards unknown or wild terrain. Many of her poems focus on rural and domestic themes, displaying empathy with the natural world and its creatures, particularly with female animals nurturing and protecting their young.

The bond with animals has been a highly consistent dimension in her writing, as we can see if we compare the following lines taken respectively from her earliest volume *The Sundial* (1978), and the more recent *Five Fields* (1998):

> I could feel the soft sucking
> Of the new-born, the tugging pleasure
> Of bruised reordering, the signal
> Of milk's incoming tide, and satisfaction
> Fall like a clean sheet around us.
>   ('Calf', CP,15)

> With a book to finish and umpteen things to do,
> here I am kneeling in straw, with a young ewe
> fussing and mothering about me, drying the lambs
> she slithered from her hot womb into the stream
> where we found them, took them for frozen or drowned.
> Working together, my hair-drier and her breath,
> we warm two shivering lambs from the brink of death.
>   ('A Very Cold Lamb', FF,18)[2]

Continuity of this kind has sometimes obscured the exploratory qualities of Clarke's writing and perhaps encouraged oversimplified critical views of her poetry as a whole. What is often concealed by the apparent familiarity of her work, and what I wish to focus on here, is arguably its most important and central characteristic, namely its persistent exploration of the often troubling yet potentially liberating boundaries of both cultural and gender identity.

I think it would be helpful at the outset to look briefly at some recent critical evaluations of Clarke's poetry which focus in particular on issues of identity. In *Ancestral Lines: Culture and Identity in the Work of Six Contemporary Poets* (1992) Linden Peach argues that the 'importance of Clarke as a Welsh poet writing in the English language is rooted to a considerable degree in the way in which she thinks of herself as a Welsh person and as a woman'.[3] He argues that it is largely through her symbolic imagery that she tries to reclaim a voice for silenced female sensibility and to stress the strengths and qualities shared by women of different historically-determined cultural contexts. Highlighting the way in which Clarke's images tend to represent all women as 'soul-mates', Peach connects this with an awareness of a 'feminine principle' in her work which has the function of reconciling opposites. A sensitive but more essentialist perspective is adopted by M. Wynn Thomas, who suggests that Clarke 'raises gender issues in terms that allow them to be ultimately subsumed within an all-embracing concept of the human', noting the importance of the 'theme of the androgynous imagination' in some of her poetry, as well as her 'refusal to polarise the sexes and to promote gender conflict'.[4]

Female critics have invariably celebrated Clarke's achievement in 'overcoming the traditional masculine bias of British poetry by giving a voice to female experience and insisting on its validity'.[5] However, while they do see qualities of dependability and integrity in her writing, they also perceive elements of conflict and ambiguity in her construction of identity and regard her as a complex poet. Llewellyn-Williams describes Clarke's *Collected Poems* as a 'rich yet shadowy book' and, while noting little evolutionary change over the years in her subject matter and style, warns that her 'accessibility may give an impression of simplicity' that is only 'skin-deep' and that she is 'anything but predictable'.[6] Comparing Clarke with Fleur Adcock and Carol Rumens, Lyn Pykett senses that 'in Clarke's 'Letter from a Far Country', there is a "submerged feminist anger in the poem's understanding of the simultaneous centrality and marginality of the women"', although ultimately the poem 'subtly changes the definition of centre and margins'.[7] Reviewing *Five Fields*, Deryn Rees-Jones welcomes the continuation of Clarke's 'exploration of a female genealogy', drawing attention to imagery of 'transformation and flux' and also considering the volume to be 'a collection of poems about journeys – journeys back not only to the past, but spiritual journeys to the rural and the urban'.[8] Indeed, in one sense Clarke has made a broadening of interests quite explicit in this volume, since the book contains two major poems written while she was a commissioned Writer in Residence at the Bridgewater Hall in Manchester.[9]

It is worth noting that, while Clarke herself does seem to recognise the generic existence of 'women's poetry', she does not regard it as synonymous with 'feminist poetry'. However, in a 1980s symposium on 'Gender in Poetry' she comments that women's poetry is often *linguistically* distinguishable from men's, not simply different in its subject matter. Clarke writes that the voices of women in the past 'were silenced, so new experience, real and our own, must resist the weight of that established aesthetic which bears so heavily on the *new language we need to express it*' and that 'If women's poetry is a new branch off the old tree, I think the clue lies in *syntax* as much as subject' [my italics].[10] Admittedly, Clarke is not very precise in defining what she means by 'language' and 'syntax' here, variously referring to 'naturalness of tone' in women's poetry, praising Sylvia Plath for telling 'the plain truth in her real voice', and commenting that words for women 'are rooted deeply in sensuous experience and can never thereafter lose their primitive force'. Furthermore, she adds that these are 'only tendencies' in women's poetry and that 'many men possess these characteristics' since 'they are part of the shift that is reshaping taste'. However, Clarke's allusion to language 'rooted deeply in sensuous experience' and 'primitive force', seems to invite analogy with an essentially Lacanian concept of Imaginary identity, which describes a mode of being pre-dating the acquisition of language or entry into the Symbolic. In Lacanian psychoanalytical thought, this entry into the Symbolic (or into the system of signifiers) coincides with the structuring of human subjectivity and the recognition of sexual difference. As feminist theorists such as Julia Kristeva have argued, the pre-linguistic or 'semiotic' stage is anarchic and thus repressed on entry into the Symbolic, though it may surface within poetic language. Like Kristeva, Clarke appears to believe that women, because they occupy a negative position in relation to discursive power and the naturalised order of the male, have a special relationship with the semiotic and privileged access to it. Clarke's view that some male poets, notably Heaney, can write in a way she would regard as characteristically female, can be compared to similar positions taken up by Virginia Woolf, as well as Kristeva and other French feminists who also believe that male writers can do this if they achieve a bisexual or androgynous imagination.[11]

My intention here is to explore through a stylistic analysis of some of Clarke's poems how the 'semiotic' in the Kristevan sense can break through to the symbolic in her writing and destabilise its meanings. Defined in broad terms, this happens when the orientational categories of her language (in particular the categories of reference, time and space, and subjectivity) begin to interrelate in a fluid, unfixed and unsettled way. A more technical term for these orientational categories is *deixis* or *deictic categories*, and before illustrating the way in which they operate in Clarke's poetry, I shall briefly define them in more formal, linguistic terms. Deictic categories are the most context-specific of all linguistic elements and the most important means by which poetic discourse, like non-poetic discourse, can 'point' to the extra-textual or 'real' world and situate the participants involved. In an article on 'Deixis and the Poetic Persona' Keith Green isolates seven deictic categories. The first, the deictic category of **Reference**, includes what he terms 'definite referring expressions; demonstrative determiners and pronouns; definite article; pronominal expressions'. Green's second category is called '**The** *origo*' and covers 'First and second person pronouns; vocatives; demonstrative adverbs; deixis encoding mental proximity/distance; honorifics'. The third category, that of **Time and space,** includes 'temporal adverbs; spatial adverbs; non-calendrical time-units (*today, next week,* etc.); tense; the concepts of *coding time, content time* and *receiving time* (and the analogous *coding place, content place,* and *receiving place*). Green explains that 'Coding time is the time at which the utterance is "transmitted"; content time is the time (or times) to which the utterance refers; and receiving time is the time when the utterance is received by the addressee or decoder'. The fourth category, **Subjectivity,** refers to the 'complexities of modality, both epistemic and deontic'.[12] Green's last two categories, **The text** and **Syntax,** are concerned respectively with what he calls 'all elements which orientate the text to itself for the reader/hearer' and with the deictic function of certain syntactic forms, such as the interrogative which 'it can be said … presupposes an addressee'.[13]

Clarke's poetry, although written in English, may include code-mixing with Welsh through reference to Welsh places and people or through the inclusion of other Welsh words and expressions, forms of address, acknowledgements, notes on translation from or allusions to Welsh literature and other documentary sources. It could be argued, I think, that **code** also has a potentially deictic function which should not be overlooked. Clarke has made frequent use of words and phrases from the Welsh language to communicate meanings in a way distinguishable as belonging to a specifically bilingual speech community. She has in fact commented on the importance of Welsh words in her poetry, saying that 'occasionally the word that comes into a poem is a Welsh one, as in one poem where I use the word "dŵr" instead of water, because it was the right one to use on that occasion'.[14] Even if many of her readers may not be able to access the meanings of the Welsh words in her poetry without the help of the notes usually provided (or even *with* the help of translation and paraphrase), Clarke still chooses to use the Welsh words in preference to possible alternatives in English because of their resonance at the level of sound symbolism or associative word senses. This choice can reinforce the deictic features of her poetry in that it reveals more about her positioning of herself in relation to her Welsh and female identity, signalling, for instance, fluctuating degrees of closeness to her cultural and familial roots, often ambivalently introducing echoes of a threatened language or a traditional patriarchal order.

The importance of the orientational categories of Clarke's poetic language can be illustrated in a number of well-known poems, but I would like to look first at a poem about her father, 'John Penri Williams (1899-1957)', which is part of the sequence 'Cofiant' from her 1989 volume *Letting in the Rumour* (reprinted in CP,121-136).[15] Finding samples of her father's handwriting in various letters and old notebooks makes the poet conscious, not just of the passing of the years since his death, but also of the way the ability to recognise his hand in an instant has remained with her. She asks 'How, after thirty years, do I know his hand?', this reflection drawing her back in time to imagine her father as a young man serving in the navy during the First World War:

> Chapel boy from Carmarthenshire
> locked in his cabin, writing home
> 'Annwyl Mam,' shocked by crew-talk,

or tapping morse as the world burned.
He drummed bad news on the sea's skin,
his air-waves singing over the roof
of the whale's auditorium. Only his heart,
the coded pulse over dark water
to a listening ship and the girl at home.

Describing her father as a 'Chapel boy from Carmarthenshire'
and using the Welsh for 'Dear Mum', Clarke associates her father
somewhat ambivalently with both a narrow-minded and Welsh-
speaking Wales as he fulfils his lonely job as a ship's radio engineer,
overwhelmed by world events and consoled only by the thought of
home and future plans. Yet the poem is not simply about the father,
but also his future daughter, Clarke herself. The poet now takes an
imaginative leap forward in time to both her own existence and the
later death of her father:

Twenty years away his daughter waits
to knock him dizzy with her birth
and scarcely twenty more
he'll strike her silent with his death,
going out on a rainy evening
in May when she isn't looking,
with a 'Hwyl fawr, Cariad.'
No message. Just, 'Over'.

It seems to me that the deictic category of time is particularly
interesting in this poem. There is quite a complex interplay between
the 'coding time' (thirty years after the father's death) and three layers
of 'content time', referring respectively to the period when Clarke's
father was on the ship, to the time of the poet's own birth twenty
years later (Clarke in fact writes 'twenty years *away*', thus merging
time and space), and to the father's death barely twenty years after
that. It is with this third layer of time, metaphorically recalling the
second layer through the words of the last line, that Clarke chooses
to end the poem, rather than with a return to the here-and-now of
her writing or coding time. Also, it is worth looking at shifts in the
deictic categories of *reference* and *the origo*, as Clarke switches from
the use of 'I' in the first stanza to refer to herself as 'she' in the third,

thus giving the impression of seeing herself as a different individual, or the 'other', in the past. Throughout the poem her father is apparently objectified and distanced through the use of 'he' rather than brought nearer through the second person pronoun or any use of vocatives. Indeed, emotional closeness seems greater the other way round, with the father addressing his daughter affectionately with the scarcely noticed 'Hwyl fawr, Cariad', translatable as 'Have fun, darling'. She, however, 'isn't looking' as he goes out of the house. By figuring her own remoteness from her father in this way, yet insisting on his devotion to her, Clarke has inscribed the poem with a problematised sense of herself as daughter and made it almost as much a confessional as elegiac text.[16] Of course we must remember that this poem was not intended to stand alone. Seen in the context of the *Cofiant* of which it is part, it also expresses a female sensibility which ultimately demands to be counted and documented. At the end of the sequence, which includes poems on a number of Clarke's female forbears, the poet reclaims the genre for the first time for the female line:

> Daughter of Penri Williams, wireless engineer of Carmarthenshire
> and Ceinwen Evans of Denbighshire
> son of William Williams, railwayman and Annie of Carmarthenshire
> son of Daniel Williams, railwayman of Llangynog and Sara...

In 'Letter from a Far Country' Clarke explores more fully what it means to be conscious of a bond with women of past generations, and here too I think a stylistic analysis can be illuminating. The poem opens with the lines 'They have gone. The silence resettles/slowly as dust on the sunlit/surfaces of the furniture', immediately suggesting how the speaker's focus is not on herself but on the family members who depend on her and also, through the simile of dust on furniture, subtly hinting too at the narrowness of the domestic perspective her role encourages her to have. Yet, now that she is alone in the house, the poet can sense her own being more intensely ('hear my blood rise and fall') and as she sets about the usual tasks of washing and cleaning she addresses 'Dear husbands, fathers, forefathers', offering them a meditation she terms 'my apologia, my/letter home from the future'.

Proud that she has done her caring job well and still taking 'pleasure counting/and listing what I have done', she tells them they 'will find all in its proper place, /when I have gone'. It is through her writing, however, that she is able to escape temporarily from the routines of homemaking and to imagine her matrilineage. As she begins to think about the traditions of female work, she quickly realises that for women of her grandmother's generation, living on any of the local farms visible from her own rural West Wales home, there were far sterner patriarchal restrictions to contend with than she has known herself ('Father and minister, on guard, / close the white gates to hold her'). The old order has been enforced not simply by specific male figures, however, but by the inherited discourses of patriarchy and the ways in which they have infiltrated education, so that in traditional tales and nursery rhymes it is almost invariably the boy who sets off for adventures and the girl who remains to 'mind things'. Clarke ambivalently acknowledges that staying behind has sometimes freed women to develop a special sensitivity to and empathy with the natural world and its creatures, an empathy which informs so many of Clarke's other poems and is perhaps her most defining characteristic. However, the natural world with which the woman empathises is not a cosy, pastoral one – indeed it seldom is in Clarke's writing. Nor is it cut off from world events. As she hangs out the washing she feels she could almost be her own grandmother 'standing/ in the great silence before the Wars', conscious of a restlessness blowing in with the sea air. The sea in fact becomes the main symbol of the poem, both representing a wider world and enacting through its perpetual rhythms the pattern of life intimately known by women ('The waves are folded meticulously, /perfectly white. Then they are tumbled/and must come to be folded again.').

A tension between praise for women as homemakers and an increasing sense of their historical powerlessness and marginalisation is sustained throughout the poem. As Clarke recalls the names of women listed as 'paupers' in the parish register or even the suicide of a woman thought to have been well-off and to lack nothing, she acknowledges that tightly-knit rural communities have in the past both neglected and misunderstood the struggles of women who were disadvantaged economically or simply unable to accept or find contentment in normalised female roles. Generations of women, 'all calling/their daughters down from the fields', to do their share of work in the home, have themselves helped to maintain the old order. The representation of motherhood has traditionally done so too, making the female gender seem to both women and men synonymous with the possession of special, intuitive responses, thus legitimating the imposition of the responsibilities for nurturing on the woman ('Children sing/that note that only we can hear.'). With the ending of the school day Clarke's meditative 'letter' must also end unfinished, as her own maternal duties call her. Interestingly, she chooses to close the poem with three italicised, rhyming quatrains in ballad-like style, apparently dismissing the possibility of escape from the traditional role ('If we adventure more than a day/Who will do the loving while we're away?'), yet this, as I hope to show, is not the acquiescence it seems to be.

Since Clarke questions female identity quite explicitly in *Letter from a Far Country* it might seem that a stylistic approach to this poem would have little to add to what can be gleaned either from the text's declarative statements or its symbolic imagery. This is not the case, however, as some attention to the deictic categories of the poem will show. First of all, I would argue that definite reference in the poem, as signalled by the definite article (e.g. 'On *the* shelves in all of *the* rooms/I arrange *the* books'), is not identical in its function to the use of such reference to denote generic concepts, as in '*The* minstrel boy to *the* war has gone./But *the* girl stays'. In the first case the reference is specific, familiar, part of the poet's immediate surroundings, whereas in the second it alludes to inherited and naturalised representations. This difference is marked further by the archaic and stylised quality of both the syntax ('to the war has gone') and the word 'minstrel'. Now this distinction is, I think, what is also foregrounded at the end of the poem with its analogous switch to a more generic type of reference ('*If we go hunting along with the men/Who will light the fires and bake bread then?*'). In present-day Western society, after all, men going hunting for survival purposes have become virtually as rare as minstrel boys, which should alert us to the danger of taking the ending of the poem too literally as a failure on Clarke's part to reach a satisfactory resolution. Lyn Pykett (1997) sees the ending as a symptom of a feminist problematic and asks whether Clarke's questions are 'meant to prod the reader into rethinking her/his views of traditional gender roles' or 'rhetorical questions intended to overwhelm the woman reader with the enormity of the problem and send her back to the safety and dry land?'.[17] I would add that the conscious shift to the ballad-like form (apparently intended, originally, to be accompanied by music, the poem being written for radio) and to generic, as opposed to specific, reference is the stylistic evidence for both this ambivalence and for Clarke's acknowledgement of the textualised nature of history. So, while Clarke appears to be saying that women must stay at home because there is no one else to do their work, she is also distancing herself from this notion by expressing it only though a clearly ritualised form in which the referential dimension is not that of her own immediate context. Another problem arising from Clarke's use of reference at the end of the poem relates to the female reader's possible resistance to the pronoun 'we'. Whereas a male reader is likely to recognise female solidarity in the use of this pronoun, the female reader will react in a less predictable way, depending on the extent to which, through her own circumstances, she may regard herself as caught between traditional female duties and personal aspirations. Clarke shows in the rest of the poem that she is aware of individualised female lives (the suicide of the woman who seemed to lack nothing), so she cannot be unconscious of the artificiality of seeing all women as automatically identifying with the role of homemaker at the end of the poem. Yet, the true closure of the poem perhaps comes just before this stylised conclusion, where Clarke pledges that when her letter is eventually finished, she will 'post it from a far country', a domain without as yet specific referentiality. However remote this prediction may appear, it is Clarke's own poem which is the principle focus here, not this as yet unknown world, as the textually deictic reference to 'this letter' makes clear. Though the letter remains unfinished it nonetheless signifies the actuality of female discourse and inevitability of social change.

As we have seen in both of the poems discussed so far, the notion of identity, whether connected to Welsh cultural roots or more specifically to a matrilineage, is not a fixed or clearly definable notion in Clarke's poetry, but one that has fluid and changing boundaries. In fact, she has quite often written poems in which the concept of identity is destabilised and undermined in one way or another. In 'Baby-sitting' she writes about the experience of finding that an instinctive maternal feeling has failed her when looking after another person's baby and that, when the baby wakes up and needs comforting, 'She will find me and between us two/It will not come. It will not come' (CP, 14). Again, in the more complex 'Cold Knap Lake' (CP, 90-91), she recalls a case of near-drowning, when a child was pulled from a lake and assumed dead until the poet's mother gave her the kiss of life and saved her. Once revived, the child was taken home by Clarke's father to a 'poor house', where she was 'thrashed for almost drowning'. Having narrated these events, the poet then asks:

> Was I there?
> Or is that troubled surface something else
> shadowy under the dipped fingers of willows
> where satiny mud blooms in cloudiness
> after the treading, heavy webs of swans
> as their wings beat and whistle on the air?

After these lines the poem ends with a couplet that transforms the particular event virtually into a folkloric myth: 'All lost things lie under closing water/in that lake with the poor man's daughter', signalling this conceptual transition in formal terms. Thus we know the poem is not so much about an actual event as about its relation to 'drowned', or nearly drowned, selves. This is in fact hinted at during the narrative part of the poem, where Clarke writes 'my mother gave a stranger's child her breath', recording her shock at this unlikely happening. The effect of the sight on Clarke as a child seems to have been one of alienation, for instead of being her parents' daughter at that moment, she was compelled to be an onlooker as another girl temporarily claimed, of necessity, their urgent response and protection. This in turn seems to have made her question subliminally the border between her own identity and that of the girl who nearly drowned, possibly in a way reminiscent of the Kristevan concept of 'abjection'[18]. A further indication of the psychological impact of the experience on Clarke is suggested through the image of the swans' intense struggle to rise off the surface of the lake, lifting themselves with difficulty from the rather sinister, 'shadowy' water towards the freedom of the air.

Poems such as 'Baby-Sitting' and 'Cold Knap Lake' show that Clarke, in spite of the strong cultural affiliations of her work, has tended to resist the notion of unitary selfhood and, perhaps increasingly, unitary nationhood as well. She has an internationalist as well as more culturally specific voice, sometimes managing to fuse the two very powerfully, as in the poem 'Neighbours' written in response to the Chernobyl disaster (CP, 85-86). Also, some of her commissioned work has broadened her writing in both thematic and formal terms, as well as allowing her the space to explore issues of identity in new ways. In 'The City' from *Five Fields* we find multi-layered and shifting images of the city of Manchester (from Roman fort to Victorian city built on the profits of Empire to today's post-industrial city of enterprise and arts) being explored alongside histories of individuals, like Clarke's own mother, who found employment there. Similarly, in 'Concerto', Clarke seems to use the underground rivers over which the new concert hall is suspended to represent the fluidity of artistic media themselves, variously illustrated in and outside the hall through commissioned sculpture and design, as well as through the music to be performed there and through Clarke's own poem. It is not the institutionalised significance of the hall that is important to her, but the fact that it appears to dissolve boundaries, to be a building at a confluence of hidden streams, to be in touch with geological as well as cultural history, to reach out beyond its physical setting to many other places, people and times. The commissioned poetry clearly contributes to what Deryn Rees-Jones in her review of *Five Fields* describes as the 'transformational quality' in this volume and shares many of the recurrent motifs of the book, including the symbolic image of ice, which 'is and is not itself, which threatens always to dissolve itself if the conditions that surround it change'.[19]

The final poem I think we should discuss in connection with

Clarke's construction of identity is 'Amber', also taken from *Five Fields*. It is worth quoting in its entirety, so that we can see in particular how its deictic language works:

> Coveted week after week on the market stall,
> coiled, nonchalant, arrayed under the lid
> of locked glass, they grew familiar.
> She'd finger them, drop them over her head,
> try them for size, spoilt for choice –
> red-amber, yellow, cut Russian ruby,
> or those sad rosaries, widow's beads of Whitby jet.
> In each bead surfaced the cloudy face of a woman.
>
> Warmed by the sunlight on dressing tables,
> or against a woman's skin, then laid safe
> in a drawer each night between the silk leaves
> of her underwear. Never cold, as if
> each bead were an unquenchable flame
> that burned a million years like a sanctuary lamp
> beneath the ice, each drip of sticky gold
> hardening to honeyed stone.
>
> As if nothing that has ever contained heat
> can be cold again, mirrors never empty
> and our rooms, furniture, hoarded amulets,
> could reassemble themselves into a life
> and still pass hand to hand from underneath
> the permafrost, ice woman to living daughter.
>   (CP, 29)

The poem is clearly an elegy, like the one that comes immediately before it in the volume and actually bears the title 'Elegy', but whereas that text is more straightforward in its reference to the poet's mother and to a moment of remembrance, 'Amber' seems to explore a complex area between grief and desire, in which the identity of the 'she' referred to in line 4 is never really represented as a mother until the last line, and only then by implication, as the 'ice-woman' who might pass on 'amulets' (jewels worn to provide protection against evil) to the 'living daughter'. The elusiveness and mysteriousness of the mother in this poem is also shown by the use of indefinite reference to her, as in 'the cloudy face of a woman' (is this the face of the woman referred to earlier, or that of an unknown woman, or even the poet herself seeing her own reflection in her mother's beads?) and 'against a woman's skin' (but which woman's skin?). The second stanza introduces an erotic tone, with its sensuous images of the warmth of the beads and of the woman's skin, the 'silk leaves/of her underwear', the passion of 'unquenchable flame' and 'burned', the sensory 'sticky gold' and 'honeyed stone'. Yet, it also contains the image of the 'sanctuary lamp/ beneath the ice', which looks forward to the 'permafrost' and 'ice-woman' of the final and much more elegiac stanza.

Like the deictic category of reference, that of time and place is also unstable in this poem. We can assume in the first line that 'the market stall' was in a town known to the poet, but within a few lines we have allusions to 'Russian ruby' and 'Whitby jet'; likewise, the temporal range of the poem includes both the trajectory of Clarke's personal memories and the 'million years' of stanza 2 and the 'ever', 'never' and 'permafrost' of the last stanza. Also, the deictic category of modality is interestingly elusive in that Clarke disguises her meanings through 'as if' clauses. When she writes 'as if/each bead were an unquenchable flame', the structure presupposes that each bead is *not* in fact so. Similarly, 'As if nothing that has ever contained heat/can be cold again' presupposes a different reality, namely that what has 'contained heat' can indeed 'be cold again'; and similarly, the mirrors *can* be 'empty' and 'our rooms, etc.' *cannot* 'reassemble themselves into a life/and still pass hand to hand…'. By choosing this kind of construction, however, Clarke not only camouflages the category of modality in the poem but at the same time opens up the possibility for the reader of resisting the presuppositions and denying their validity, in other words of breaking momentarily free of the logic of the contingent world. The modality we are left with is not that of impossibility after all, but of tenuous possibility. There is a sense of continuation in this poem in just the same way as there is in the much earlier poem 'Lunchtime Lecture', in which, seeing the skeleton of a female 'from the second or third millennium/B.C.', Clarke describes the ancestral woman as 'a tree in winter' and herself as 'the tree/Fleshed' (CP, 20-21).

It is worth remembering, when we consider Clarke's writing

overall, that for most of the twentieth century Welsh poetry in English
was dominated by male writers. Even in 1975 an influential anthology
could omit women writers altogether and claim without any apparent
self-doubt that 'Anglo-Welsh poetry is poetry written in English by
Welshmen or by non-Welshmen who have made Wales the basis of
their inspiration' and that 'essentially it illuminates what it means to
be a Welshman in the twentieth century'.[20] Such naturalised
patriarchal assumptions underpinned the cultural climate in which
Clarke first began to publish her poetry. Yet, in a relatively short
space of time, she succeeded in feminising the traditional subjects of
rural life and nostalgia for one's roots (the Welsh *hiraeth*), also finding
wider and sometimes internationalist perspectives on Welsh culture.
In this chapter I have tried to show by looking closely at the
orientational categories of her poetic language that Gillian Clarke
has essentially constructed a sense of identity and selfhood that, while
respectful of the cultural and literary legacy handed down to her, refuses
to be closed in by it and remains essentially exploratory and provisional.
Today it is, I think, clearer than ever how much terrain she has in this
way reclaimed for the female sensibility, which other women poets in
Wales and elsewhere can inhabit and explore in their turn.[21]

NOTES
[1] Menna Elfyn, ed. *Trying the Line*: a Volume of Tribute to Gillian Clarke
(Llandysul: Gomer, 1997), 8-9.
[2] 'Calf' originally had the title 'Birth' in The Sundial (Llandysul: Gomer, 1978).
Both *Collected Poems* (1997) and *Five Fields* (1998) were published by
Carcanet, Manchester.
[3] Linden Peach, *Ancestral Lines: Culture and Identity in the Work of Six
Contemporary Poets* (Bridgend: Seren, 1992), 76-94.
[4] M. Wynn Thomas, *Corresponding Cultures: The Two Literatures of Wales*
(Cardiff: University of Wales Press 1999),186-202.
[5] Hilary Llewellyn-Williams, 'Rooms of the Mind: Gillian Clarke's Collected
Poems', *Poetry Wales*, vol.34, no.2. (October 1998), 16-19.
[6] Llewellyn-Williams, 16-19.
[7] Lyn Pykett, 'Women Poets and "Women's Poetry": Fleur Adcock, Gillian
Clarke and Carol Rumens', in *British Poetry from the 1950s to the 1990s*,
eds. Gary Day and Brian Docherty (London: Macmillan, 1997), 253-267.

[8] Deryn Rees-Jones, *Poetry Wales*, vol 35, no.2 (October, 1999),61-62.

[9] 'The City' and 'Concerto' were first broadcast on Radio 3 in 1997.

[10] *Planet 66*, Dec/Jan1987-88: 60-61.

[11] For a more detailed account of these issues see Sara Mills, 'The Gendered Sentence', in *The Feminist Critique of Language: A Reader*, ed. Deborah Cameron (London and New York: Routledge,1998), 65-77.

[12] 'Modality' refers to the ways in which the meaning of a proposition may be modified by the presence of modal auxiliary verbs such as 'can', 'must' or 'should', or through other ways of expressing possibility, certainty, etc.. Epistemic modality expresses a judgement about whether a proposition is true or possible, probable etc., whereas deontic modality involves the expression of permission or obligation.

[13] Keith Green, 'Deixis and the Poetic Persona', Language and Literature, vol. 1, no.2 (1992),121-134.

[14] This remark is quoted and commented on in Peach (1992:84-85), who tells us that Clarke is alluding specifically to the poem 'The Water-Diviner' which has been compared to Heaney's 'The Diviner'. Peach draws attention to different emphases in the two poems, arguing that Clarke is closer than Heaney to the rural area she is writing about and adding: 'Heaney's poem closes with the movement of the stick in the Diviner's grasp, following the failure of members of the crowd who watch to get the same results themselves. Clarke's poem, on the other hand, closes with the gush of water: "dŵr...dŵr...dŵr". It is expressed appropriately in Welsh because the sound of the repetition of the Welsh-language word better conveys the movement of the water than the English-language 'water' would have done. Also the use of the Welsh language here reflects the way in which the mystical skills of the Diviner were better understood and appreciated in the older, Welsh-language, rural culture.'

[15] In her introduction to the sequence Clarke makes it clear she is adopting a genre associated with the patriarchal order: '*Cofiant* means biography. In Wales the tradition of the *Cofiant* developed in the nineteenth century when many hundreds were written, mainly about preachers. They usually included an account of the subject's life, a selection of his sermons, letters and other writings and ended with tributes and an elegy.'

[16] In this connection it is interesting to note that Clarke has distinguished between the way men, and male poets, tend to see themselves in terms of objective roles, and the way women 'often move halfway into a role, the transition incomplete and felt rather than seen.... Certainly they show a markedly greater interest in the detail and subtlety of relationships'. ('Hunter-gatherer or madonna mistress?', *Bloodaxe Catalogue*, 1986-7, 20.)

[17] Pykett, 265.

[18] Julia Kristeva, *Powers of Horror: an Essay on Abjection* (1980) (New York: Columbia University Press, 1982), 4. Here Kristeva writes that abjection is caused by '...what disturbs identity, system, order. What does not respect borders, positions, rules. The in-between, the ambiguous, the composite.

The traitor, the liar …Any crime, because it draws attention to the fragility of the law, is abject…'. In Clarke's poem the horror associated with the near-drowning and the 'crime' of the way in which the girl was treated on being taken home, as well as the poet's own sense of the disruption to her sense of herself as her parents', and particularly her mother's, child, could all be said to bring about abjection in this text.

[19] Deryn Rees-Jones, 61-62.

[20] Don Dale-Jones and Randal Jenkins, eds., *Twelve Modern Anglo-Welsh Poets* (London: University of London Press, 1975),13.

[21] Some of these poets are interestingly discussed by Francesca Rhydderch in '"Between my tongue's borders": contemporary Welsh women's poetry', *Poetry Wales*, vol.33, no.4 (April 1998), 39-45.

Liberating Mercury: The Poems of Edwin Morgan

Paul Mills

Building worlds

One of the pleasures of reading stories and poems in any age is that of being able to enter the world the writer has built up for us. The writer invites us to enter it as newcomers, as though we are discovering it for ourselves. Edwin Morgan offers his readers this kind of invitation. An important thing to appreciate about his writing is how each of his poems builds a world, opens doorways, lets us in. But what happens then? He doesn't tell us what we should think or how we ought to respond once we are there. He is elusive and shape-shifting like quicksilver or mercury. Applied to a person the word 'mercurial' means swift, changeable, hard to pin down to a fixed set of opinions. It also suggests something perhaps magical.

In writing this piece I am trying to discover what Edwin Morgan's poems might be about. I don't intend to dig into his background. He is Scottish, born in 1920, and has lived all his life in Glasgow. Before he retired he taught literature at Glasgow University. His first book of poems was published in 1952, his latest, *New Selected Poems,* in 2000. In March of that year he was awarded the Queen's Gold Medal for Poetry, a considerable honour which few poets have achieved. But that is enough and all we need to know. His collection of essays on poetry, with some on translation (he is also a prolific translator of poems from several European languages) appeared in 1974. It is his poems and essays that I shall investigate.

Although his poems don't seem to contain an obvious message, this isn't to say they are free of attitude. Almost always we are hearing the tone of a speaking voice, sometimes a range of voices. And many of his poems have a dramatic quality – there is an encounter;

something *happens*. Readers are enabled to think for themselves, entertained, sometimes shocked. In no way are we coerced by mere information. If we hear a dry voice of authority and instruction, this will be often countered by another – a bewildered voice somehow off-course and not so able to reach confident conclusions. The Morgan attitude is one of resistance to fixed and prescriptive opinions. Bewilderment in his work is a positive sign, and is so because of its openness to other positive signs – joy, surprise, sympathy, discovery.

Science and cities

Morgan is sometimes described by reviewers as a poet whose subject is science. Maybe that's one way of pinning him down. But Morgan's conception of science remains ambivalent, questioning, and in this way reflects an attitude relevant to his practice as a poet. On the one hand contemporary science – astrophysics, space exploration, computers – illustrates an attempt to close the world, to fix it into a series of observable cause-and-effect laws, organise it for forms of exploitation. Deep space and particle physics tell our own contemporary creation story, or this is their aim. On the other hand science builds strange, imaginary futures, opens up our minds to curiosity, starts to tear our understood world apart, challenges our language of the familiar. In other words science poses a question to us about how we make meaning – through closed systems or open ones, through rules and laws or imagination.

Edwin Morgan began to pick up these issues and examine them quite early in his writing. Somehow poetry wasn't the place for them, or hadn't been, or so it was thought. In 1963, he wrote on the subject of science:

> Why has the modern poet contributed so little? 'It is bizarre', said C. P. Snow in his Rede Lecture *The Two Cultures and the Scientific Revolution,* 'how very little of twentieth century science has been assimilated into twentieth century art.' And whatever reservations one may have about that lecture, Snow's implied and stated criticisms of modern poets are well justified. If it is not the duty, it should at least be the delight, of poets to contemplate the world of science. It is only indeed by an extraordinary ingrownness and wilful self-blinkering that

modern poetry has managed to preserve its purity from contamination by the dominant interest of the age ... Science and art may not yet be one flesh – but has an engagement not been announced? (CE p17,19)

In his collection *From Glasgow to Saturn* (1973) he reiterated that announcement, and in his *New Selected Poems*, written in his eightieth year, Morgan continues to celebrate that relationship, not least through the inclusion of his sequence of poems 'Planet Wave', covering the history of the Earth from the Big Bang to the time of Copernicus.

In the same way as students of Milton might ask 'Who was Lucifer?' or 'Who was Comus?' and feel they need a background knowledge of the Bible or classical myth to explain his allusions, now they are increasingly likely to encounter references to science. 'Who was Copernicus?' is a question of importance to our *present* understanding of the world, for it was Copernicus who, even before Galileo invented the telescope, discovered that the Earth and planets move around the Sun. After Copernicus, writing in the sixteenth century, science began to replace religion as the testament of reality.

In the last section of 'Planet Wave' Morgan himself attempts to realise more accurately who Copernicus was:

> Who was he, and does it matter? No stories
> are told about this man who kicked the earth
> from its false throne ... He had servants,
> rode a horse, healed the sick, heard cases,
> administered a province, but his big big eyes
> smouldered like worlds still unadministered ...

One such world of course was the planet Mercury, closest to the sun in the solar system – here 'still unadministered', and (we can almost hear Morgan saying) long may it remain so. There's something mercurial too about Copernicus ('Who was he, and does it matter?'). Asking the same question about Edwin Morgan, all we get are some details – not much more. And, as for 'worlds still unadministered', science reveals them, but will it also result in the conquest of them?

If we think of what has happened in science in our own time, say in the last six decades of the twentieth century, the list is amazing, as well as perhaps worrying: nuclear fission, nuclear power, Hiroshima, DNA and genetic modification, computers, the Moon landing, the Hubble telescope with its photographs of galaxies billions of light-years away from Earth, the discovery of our earliest human ancestors, instruments scanning the heavens for alien life, climate change transforming our view of the future. So Morgan is right. Science is altering not only our practical everyday-life experience but also affecting our deepest comprehensions of our world. How can these *not* be the subject of poetry?

Morgan's own view of what poetry is and what it can do supports the idea that poetry needs to respond to the contemporary. When I was a student at Edinburgh University in the mid 1960s, one gloomy Sunday afternoon in October I set off to explore my new surroundings. My map of the city looked interesting – down some roads near where I lived in Comely Bank Road was the coast. When I got there I found Silverknowes Park – high-rise flats and a desperate, bleak shoreline – not what I was expecting. The sea, too, was grey and uneventful, somehow abandoned. To me this was different from anything in England. Nothing was happening here. It was a void. And yet these were the very locations – the schemes – about which Irvine Welsh would be writing twenty or so years later in *Trainspotting*. He could have been one of the kids I saw in the street, doing nothing because there was nothing to do.

At that time, although I didn't know it, Edwin Morgan was making a point about the state of literature in Scotland: that it wasn't keen to address the present, wasn't willing to get up close to experience, was lost somewhere in its idealised past, through which it continued to form its identity. Four years before my own brief impression of 'the schemes' at Silverknowes, he was writing:

> I am certain that Scottish Literature is being held back, and young writers are slow to appear, not only because of a prevailing intellectual mood of indifferentism and conservatism, a desperate unwillingness to move out into the world with which every child at school is becoming familiar – the world of television and sputniks, automation and LPs, electronic music and multistorey flats, rebuilt city centres and new towns,

> coffee bars and bookable cinemas, air travel and transistor
> radios, colour-photography and open-plan houses, paperbacks
> and water-skiing, early marriage and larger families: a world
> that will be more fast, more clean, more 'cool' than the one it
> leaves behind. How ridiculous to list distinguishing features
> of contemporary culture – material ones at that! Yet material
> differences in society imply spiritual, moral, and aesthetic
> differences, and although writers can struggle for a time on
> language, on myth, on nature, on 'eternal emotions', there
> comes a day of reckoning when they realise that they are not
> speaking the same terms as their audience. (CE, p175)

It is the terms, values and speech of the people, *their* stories, their
world of new and fantastic commodities, which he is arguing should
be recorded, responded to, not sifted out and ignored by so-called
Literature. And so we can see in this extract something of the drift
and range of his sympathies as a poet. We can also see these as not
that different from his interest in science. There is in both a need to
address the idiom, drive and language of the contemporary, to listen,
take note of, and learn from what is happening, to see the gaps and
inhibitions in his own national literature.

A little plastic model of the solar system

To focus our minds on the published texts of his poems, we need a
sense of the different and various pressures he is negotiating, his need
to build up recognisable worlds while also dealing in terms which
seem comparatively unfamiliar in poetry – terms which make
reference to lunar modules, aliens and computers, as well as to
Glasgow streets and high-rise blocks, both the urban present and the
futuristic, the science fact and science fiction subject, and the actual
visited streets of the real. His territories are wide and unconfined and
many of them involve language itself. As a translator he understands
the speaking of different worlds. The urge to blend, unify and
incorporate is balanced by a need to celebrate variety, to strengthen
community while preserving difference and independence. All of this
calls for negotiation.

His poem 'The First Men on Mercury' published in 1973
illustrates what looks like a coalescence, an attempt at a cohabiting

of languages. Opposing forces meet. On the one hand there are the colonisers from Earth, possibly wishing to plant their flag of conquest yet appearing to speak a language of peace and friendship. On the other there are the inhabitants of Mercury. We hear the invaders from Earth speaking first:

> – We come in peace from the third planet.
> Would you take us to your leader?
>
> – Bawr stretter! Bawr. Bawr. Stretterhawl?
>
> – This is a little plastic model
> of the solar system, with working parts.
> You are here and we are there and we
> are now here with you, is this clear?
>
> – Gawl horrop. Bawr. Abawrhannahanna!
>
> – Where we come from is blue and white
> with brown, you see we call the brown
> here 'land', the blue is 'sea', and the white
> is 'clouds' over land and sea, we live
> on the surface of the brown land,
> all round is sea and clouds. We are 'men'.
> Men come –
>
> – Glawp men! Gawrbenner menko. Menhawl?
>
> – Men come in peace from the third planet
> which we call 'earth'. We are earthmen.
> Take us earthmen to your leader.
>
> – Themen? Thmen? Bawr. Bawrhossop.
> Yuleeda tan hanna. Harrabost yuleeda.
>
> – I am the yuleeda. You see my hands,
> we carry no benner, we come in peace.
> The spaceways are all stetterhawn.
>
> – Glawn peacemen all horrabhanna tantko!
> Tan come at'mstrossop. Glawp yuleeda! (NSP p 69)

A meeting, and, up to this point, not very promising or auspicious. Will it get better? As readers we try to interpret the tone and mood of the Mercurians. ('Gawl. Horrop') It doesn't sound too friendly. But what about the mood and speech of the earthmen? Can we interpret that with any certainty? Their model of the solar system 'with working parts', their persistent reference to leaders and to leadership, their talking-down-to-the-natives approach to interplanetary relations – all these suggest assumptions of high status, superior knowledge, power over inferiors, even while they persistently seem to be talking about peace.

Notice how the natives' interruptions aren't listened to but dismissed and ignored. Why do men say 'we come in peace' if not to conceal some other, sinister, and all too probable motive? Resistant to conquest, suspicious of these enforcers, the Mercurian speech seems considerably easier to interpret. The exchange of words from one language to the other does not alleviate but simply strengthens the impression of aggressive difference as the conversation progresses. The earthmen have a spokesman 'I am the yuleeda'. Rank appears to count in the 'earth' language.

In an address by Edwin Morgan at the opening of a writing conference in Glasgow in 1991 he made reference to the NASA moon landing:

> If we are backward, backward in our social and political organisation, so that it was impossible for us to send a United Nations rocket for the first moon landing, instead of (as happened) having the Stars and Stripes planted in the lunar dust, like an atavistic sign of conquest (and that remains true, despite the astronaut's remark about 'a giant leap for mankind'), if we are still so bound by feelings of territory and domination that we take a national flag to the moon, is this a good thing or a bad thing? Are we really all that backward, or on the contrary is this how evolution proceeds, through diversity, endless diversity with all its attendant dangers and difficulties? These are basic questions. (CH p1-2).

Morgan's address here raises the same issues as the poem. An invasive culture indicates lack of enlightened progress, surely, and yet he is able to take a step forward or beyond, and to consider the long-distance view. Diversity can be seen as good, and bad. So should we condone the US flag planted on the Moon's surface (or on Mercury's)? Or should we deplore it? Whose side are we on? The earthmen's or the Mercurians? The mercurial poet won't let us be certain. Is it possible to be on both sides at once? In the poem it is the

Mercurians who have the last say:

> – You men we know bawrhossoptant. Bawr.
> We know yuleeda. Go strawng backspetter quick.
> (NSP p 69-70)

No doubt about it. This is not friendship or peace but predatory assertion, and so must be resisted. But conquest might be part of evolution, might be one of the features of our evolutionary diversity. The poem might be doing no more than witnessing those 'attendant dangers and difficulties' diversity and conquest bring with them. How many times and in what other circumstances have conquerors behaved in exactly this way? coming in so-called 'peace' to invade native populations, attempting some cursory, opportunist practice of their language? The instances in our own planet's history are numberless, and for this reason I think that most readers will feel pleased that the earthmen, along with their crude scientific models and ideas of leadership, get told where to go.

This poem illustrates another of Morgan's qualities as a poet. His fascination is with words as sound, as shape, as if language itself were a kind of substance, pliable, flexible, plastic. His experiments with concrete poems, for example, are visible attempts at a form of verbal recycling. A concrete poem is a machine for the recycling of language. Words going in in one combination come out in another. The process of recycling operates endlessly, seems almost unstoppable. Language appears constantly reusable, possessed of the same mercurial spirit as the poet, susceptible to invention and re-invention. Each solid, permanent-looking shape on the page is an illusion disguising a state of shifting possibility, continuous transformation.

But the main point is that a poem like 'The First Men on Mercury' isn't intended to resolve the wider question of how and why species and nations evolve. The poem could be read as a version of the English infiltration of Scotland. But in terms of its text it simply dramatises some of these issues for us, invites us in, does not seek to motivate us in any special direction. The earthmen might in this instance have been seen off, but it's clear from Morgan's address in 1991 that the issues remain open in his mind. They remain open as basic questions, not as basic answers. The poet's mind is focused intensely on the immediate drama of the encounter, yet is standing back, cool, 'mercurial'.

Even so, despite such dramatisations, it might be possible to detect Morgan's underlying sympathies, his drift. And it does seem in this poem there is a drift or a gist. Surely we ought to be rising above our urge to plant our flag, to resist subscribing yet again to that unprogressive, pugilistic history. Sharply dramatised poems like 'The First Men on Mercury' draw us inevitably to the question – What does he think? What's his stance, his position? Can we deduce it? Is it simply a discourse of open questions? Is there something trackable through the range and scope of his writing?

Romantic uncertainty: 'The Needle's Point'

In the last two decades Morgan's writing has developed a sense of affirmation, has moved away from conflict towards the fascinated discovery of new worlds for poetry.

> In the most awesome of all his pictures he builds up the vast prospect of mountain-tops, clouds, moon, and stars, seen like another sea stretching out of Snowdon into the Atlantic main, while from below he hears the roaring of torrents mounting up into the calm. The mountain, with all the forms of clouds and waters surrounding and washing it, is his symbol of 'a majestic intellect' raised far above (but still a part of) the plain of ordinary feeling. (CE pp 127-8)

This wonderfully descriptive passage is taken from an essay by Edwin Morgan written in 1957 about Wordsworth's poem *The Prelude*. But it could almost be about Morgan's own writing thirty or forty years later – the sense of space, of wonder in the presence of wild landscape. I say 'almost' because, unlike Wordsworth, with Morgan's poems we don't get a sense of a towering 'majestic intellect' rising above 'the plain of ordinary feeling'. That image of remote towering belongs to poets of the Romantic period, like Wordsworth, also like Coleridge who wrote with similar awe about Mont Blanc. Edwin Morgan never abandons his sense of ordinary feeling, or subjects his readers to the kind of religious encounter with landscape favoured by the Romantics. If there is a type of Romantic in him, it is one that keeps his mind focused closely onto the actual matter of the world rather than on some 'transcendent power', to use Wordsworth's phrase. Here, in *Sonnets from Scotland* (1984) is Morgan's description of ice sheets retreating across the Grampian highlands:

Post-Glacial

The glaciers melt slowly in the sun.
The ice groans as it shrinks back to the pole.
Loud splits and cracks send shudders through the shoal
of herring struggling northwards, but they run
steadily on into the unknown roads
and the whole stream of life runs with them. Brown
islands hump up in the white of land, down
in the valleys a fresh drained greenness loads
fields like a world first seen, and when mild rains
drive back the blizzards, a new world it is
of grain that thrusts its frenzied spikes, and trees
whose roots race under the stamped-out remains
of nomad Grampian fires. Immensities
are mind, not ice, as the bright straths unfreeze.

(SS NSP p 131)

If the rhythm of the verse derives partly from Wordsworth, the action it depicts almost never veers from geological exactness informed by science. There's just a hint, at the end, of an older Romanticism – 'Immensities/are mind' – though that mind is more the mind of the scientist-poet than the Romantic philosopher. The observer doesn't put himself in the picture, or attempt to influence its significance beyond showing *what is,* or *what is seen.* The emphasis here is on 'unknown roads … a world first seen … new worlds.' Like science, poetry can go anywhere – into the past, into the far-off future. It can travel to the moons of Jupiter, listen in to voices from distant planets. It can put us in touch with a Scotland as it was hundreds of thousands of years ago as well as in the present, and it can do all this in a mood of 'delight' – Morgan's word for the poet's response to science. Here is another example of 'delight' from the poem 'On the Needle's Point' (1982):

Of course it is not a point at all.
We live here and we should know.
I doubt indeed if there can be a point
in created things; the finest honing
uncovers more rough. Our ground stretches
for several miles; it is like living
on a asteroid, a bounded island
but with a bottomless core lost in mist
so far below and out of sight we feel
like pillar saints in earthly Syria ...
We have had some climbing over and down
with home-made crampons, disappearing
perhaps making it to what we cannot imagine ...
But I like it on the point, good
is the dark cavern, good the craggy walks,
good the vertiginous bare brightness,
good the music, good the dance
when sometimes we join wings and drift
in interlinking circles, how many thousands
I could never tell, silent ourselves,
almost melting into light. (NSP p 120)

The 'point' is a place – Earth, or somewhere similar. (How much more interesting and mysterious he makes it than the Earthmen's model: 'bits of white with brown'.) But any attempt to give it a point, that is, a purpose, fails, 'uncovers more rough'. Does life need to have a purpose? Like Jehovah in The Book of Genesis, Morgan is seeing the world and that it is 'good' That suffices him. Communities, harmonies, music and dance are possible; they exist. Do they need a reason? Explorations might lead us towards 'what we cannot imagine'. Knowledge is partial. Could it ever be otherwise? The 'interlinking circles' of joined wings might be happening somewhere, or nowhere, surrounded by the unknown and 'lost in mist'. If we think of Wordsworth again on Snowdon – another kind of needle's point – Morgan's position is one of Romantic *un*-certainty. The poet is in a state of being out of touch with anything like Wordsworth's resolving truths – And so be it. In this he reflects the condition of modern writing, possessing no plastic model with working parts designed for conquest, inhabiting a world permanently inexplicable, addicted not to the vision but to the glimpse.

Dancing with chaos: 'Cinquevalli'

What this point suggests, however, is that Morgan, in choosing subjects to write about, operates with an unrestricted licence. He writes about whatever supports and nourishes his delight. In this sense he is mercurial. He's like a performer constantly changing shape before our eyes, inventing new acts with elastic speed, in some secret pact with expressive chaos. He write eloquently and with approval of the performer Cinquevalli, the Polish trapeze artist who fell to the floor of a circus ring in St Petersburg only to re-invent himself later as a expert juggler. I choose the term 're-invent' for its literal meaning – 're-inhalation, taking in new air'. Finally, in London, his coffin-bearers face the juggler's challenge:

> Cinquevalli's coffin sways through Brixton
> only a few months before the Armistice.
> Like some trick they cannot get off the ground
> it seems to burden the shuffling bearers, all their arms
> cross-juggle that displaced person, that man
> of balance, of strength, of delights and marvels,
> in his unsteady box at last into the earth. (NSP p 129)

Even though Cinquevalli fought against gravity, and lost, this poem powerfully celebrates his urge to defy its laws, to belong to chaos, to be 'displaced'. Morgan invents Cinquevalli as a performer of the impossible: 'After eight years perfecting / he can balance one billiard ball on another billiard ball / on top of a cue on top of a third billiard ball / in a wine-glass held in his mouth.' His act is a series of metaphors for the creative: the art of balancing objects in impossible relationships, linking them in ways which seem impossible, and which by defying gravity proves its truth. Where would Cinquevalli be *without* gravity? As with jugglers, as with poets, an opposing force needs to be there in order to supply the full, performative mystery of the act. The audience asks: 'How did you do that? What holds them (words, objects) together?' And the answer – 'After eight years perfecting'. Harmony, balance, control – and yet chaos, and yet possible stumbling – up there in space yet the possible fall never more than an eyelid-flicker away.

In Morgan's speech at the writing conference in Glasgow, here too we find a similar sense of anxiety and delight in the practice of art. A circle, he begins by explaining, is a symbol of power, harmony, coherence. But what of the maze? This too is another potent symbol. Again revealing his love of performance and mercurial energy, he recreates these symbols as types of dance:

> I mentioned earlier the importance of dancing in a circle, but in mediaeval times people used also to dance through a maze, which is a less obvious but more interesting thing to do. Both the circle dance and the maze dance were thought to be symbolic of something universal in their different ways. And in the most symbolic dance of all, the profound and wonderful dance of the Dervishes in Turkey, each dancer spins in a circle, with arms outstretched, the left palm facing downwards to embrace the earth and the right palm facing upwards to embrace the heavens, and each dancer spins in his own time, not in unison with the other dancers (though obviously it is a group activity), like the planets of our solar system which we now know are extraordinarily varied, in ways that so far defy logical development or evolution. If you can imagine someone looking down from above on a dance of Dervishes, it would be like the movement of fundamental particles, in the sense that you could never predict exactly where any one dancer would be in relation to the others. And yet some force does hold them together. A nice image of what physicists now call chaos.
>
> So is the world a circle or a labyrinth? Geometry or chaos? (CH p 4)

If we make the attempt to summarise in a logical way the evolution of Edwin Morgan's poetry, we could find ourselves gazing at particles, unpredictable, 'yet some force does hold them together.' Poems are planets, or Dervishes, each of them defying logical development yet held by the same force – each of them, too, performing a circle dance or a dance of mazes, facing this way and that, and yet with a secret preference for the chaotic. Or can we be sure? Ultimately it may be in the constantly surprising tension between circle and maze, unity and variety, that these poems are able to develop life. Morgan's theme in his lecture extends to language. Does the future look likely to see the development of one world, one language?

> The vision of one world, with the concomitant vision of one language, will never disappear, but in practice the last fifty or sixty years have seen just as much interest taken in language difference as in the search for a universal grammar, and the tension or dialectic between the two approaches seems to me healthy and productive. (CH p 7).

Even so, it can firmly be said that if Morgan's poems are any guide to the future, no 'one world, one language' is ever going to be found in his utopia. Oneness behaves more like the law of gravity. As with Cinquevalli it exists only to be defied. His commitment all through is to re-invention, re-exhilaration. He really doesn't like that plastic model with moving parts. His preference is for the new wind of uncertainty, for chaos – in science, and in poetry too. Geometry or chaos? He needs both. The world is both labyrinth and circle, geometry and maze. The worlds he builds in his poems acknowledge both, but with a strong bias towards the mercurial. If, like Cinquevalli, one thing doesn't work he can suddenly change, aim to reinvent himself elsewhere.

Gripping the real: 'Christmas Eve', 'In the Snack-bar'

Before going on to discuss his latest sequence 'Planet Wave', I would like to take a step back to an earlier poem 'Christmas Eve', first published in From Glasgow to Saturn but excluded from his *New Selected Poems*. Far from the scene of traditional Christmas Eves, but passing lighted windows in the streets, the poem's action takes place on the upper deck of a bus. The poet sits down next to a scruffy young man in white jeans. He notices this man's hands:

> tattooed on the four fingers ADEN 1967
> and on the right hand five Christian crosses.
> As the bus jerked, his hand fell on my knee,
> stayed there, lay heavily and alive
> with blue carvings from another world
> and seemed to hold me like a claw,

> unmoving. It moved. I rubbed my ear
> to steal a glance from him, found him
> stealing a glance at me. It was not
> the jerking of the bus, it was a proposition.
>   (GTS p 86)

In the minds of Morgan's generation, Aden signified disputed territory on the Asian shore of the Red Sea. The young man's age, and 1967, suggests might have had something to do with a recent threat of war in that area. Whether or not, the association of Aden with danger, violence, conflict, as well as with the remotely exotic, would have been unmistakeable. Fascinating to Morgan at that moment, the tattooed hands advertise deep connections with such experiences. The next minute 'our eyes held / while that blue hand burned into my leg.' The proposition is sexual. Rejected or refused? We never find out because the conductor (authority) intervenes. But not before this man has made his proposition explicit: 'Don't ge' aff tae ah ge' aff.'. What happens? 'Christmas Day' was published in the mid sixties – a period when homosexual acts were judged to be criminal in law and the mind of society.

> My ticket was up, I had to leave him sprawled there
> with that hand that seemed now so defenceless
> lying on the seat I had left. Half down the stair
> I looked back. The last thing I saw was Aden
> and five blue crosses for five dead friends.

But we can't blame the conductor, or the ticket. The speaker of the poem *wants* to escape – not because he doesn't find the proposition exciting – he might – but because, like Cinquevalli, he must defy its gravity. Its social implications are too serious, bringing with them a sense of real consequences. And so his mercurial spirit won't submit. It is this finally which refuses. As a poet he must resist the heavy downward pressure of that clawlike hand. Its gripping weight, imprinted with death and war and the names of friends unbalances him. Its urgent strength and dependency point downward, like the left hand of a Dervish. He must counter it by getting away. So he escapes, and not without a sense of regret breathes freely, leaving his own defenselessness behind.

If the mercurial poet needs to escape, the poem's style like a dog on a leash can't stop sniffing at what is in front of its nose. It is fixated and will not be pulled away. It won't let go of that hand, just as the hand itself won't let go. More space is given to that hand – its tattoos, position, grip – than to any other instance or thing. There is a tension, yet somehow we know this happened, wasn't just fabricated. Not just a memory but some kind of trace experience has entered Morgan's imagination and stayed with him. It has that intensity of re-created detail, and is therefore able to enter the imagination of readers. The language twines itself around the experience. He is – against his will – bound by it.

The poem's opening descriptive sequence: 'Streaming cars all dark with parcels', suggests documentary, incidental recall. Stars like Christmas lights. Lights like stars. But these are the only metaphors. The scene unfolds, produces the experience in close-up, in its immediacy. He lets it go only after a long and regretful look in its direction. In other words he has been both physically and imaginatively 'gripped'. This poem too alerts us to the other life of the city, to something concealed under the macho surface of Scottish culture. The inclusion of speech is a shock. Like the poet we are forced into some entanglement with the actual. Like him we don't know how to react, nor will the working models of Christmas Eves, heterosexual, normalising and conquering, give us any clue to the reality.

This type of close-up, vivid-impression style, immediate re-creation of scene and character, belongs to an earlier period of Morgan's writing. It happens again in the poem 'In the Snack-bar', where the poet acting on a sudden compassionate impulse helps an old blind hunchback to get to the gents:

> A few yards of floor are like a landscape
> to be negotiated, in the slow setting out
> time has almost stopped. I concentrate
> my life to his: crunch of spilt sugar,
> slidy puddle from the night's umbrellas,
> table edges, people's feet,
> hiss of the coffee machine, voices and laughter,

> smell of a cigar, hamburgers, wet coats steaming,
> and the slow dangerous inches to the stairs.
> I put his right hand on the rail
> and take his stick. He clings to me. The stick
> is in his left hand, probing the treads.
> I guide his arm and tell him the steps.
> And slowly we go down. And slowly we go down …
>   (NSP p 32)

The poem lists objects to be negotiated 'like a landscape'. Everything, no matter how slightly or randomly adjacent – 'table edges, people's feet' – is a problem for this blind old man. Even 'the hiss of the coffee machine, voices and laughter' are hurdles, edges, as if laughter itself could trip him up. Without help he won't make it through this space where everything is an obstruction. And for a few minutes during which Morgan inhabits this defenceless old man's angle towards the world, he too is living in touch with objects, impressions, sounds, each of which is immediate, clinging, and in treacherous close-up. 'He clings to me' – just like the young man did in 'Christmas Eve'.

'Christmas Eve' and 'In the Snack-bar' show how Morgan learned his craft as a poet – how to focus his mind so closely on those who are his subjects he seems to become enveloped by their reality. But his writing wasn't going to remain there. This helpless empathy with the defenceless, while not revoked (Morgan retains throughout his work a deep sense of predicaments), still needed to give some ground to imaginative drives pulling in other directions. The right-hand palm of the dancer pointed upward, and in other poems his realist style unwraps itself from earthbound subjects and moves in a broader sweep. But only so far. Sometimes these opposites unbalance. If Cinquevalli typifies the infinitely buoyant and mercurial human being, in the following lines his self-inventions are starting to grind down:

> Cinquevalli broods in his armchair in Brixton Road.
> He reads in the paper about the shells whining
> at Passchendale, imagines the mud and the dead.
> He goes to the window and wonders through that dark evening
> what is happening in Poland where he was born.

His neighbours call him a German spy.
'Kestner. Paul Kestner, that's his name!'
'Keep Kestner out of the British music-hall!'
He frowns; it is cold; his fingers seem stiff and old. (NSP p 128)

Like the young man in 'Christmas Eve' and the old man in the snack-bar, Cinquevalli here is trapped by 'mud and the dead', by an identity not self-made but forced on him by others and by history, locked in a world of mockery and opinions, also of irreducable facts.

Lift off: 'Planet Wave'

The mercurial flight was still to be found, and came with 'Planet Wave'. Although not 'music-hall' exactly, this sequence was commissioned by the Cheltenham International Festival and performed with a jazz accompaniment in Cheltenham Town Hall in April 1977. Reading it you need to imagine the music. The speaker is an observer. His stance is detached. And yet his record of the events becomes increasingly moved and moving. The poetry flows out in exciting, unpredictable rhythms, its tone light, dark, comic, inquisitive. It starts with the creation of matter and ends in praise of Copernicus (Who was Copernicus?). The science learned by Morgan is accompanied by his visions (glimpses) of history. There's no God. His imagination transforms into reality whatever has been learned or glimpsed through science. His language can wrap itself round some small thing, and can also move on – has to move on. Pace is everything: Earth and World are being born, delivered by the showman shaman poet. Almost as soon as Man appears, he's drunk:

> I joined them for their meal. They had a bard,
> a storyteller, just like me, I said.
> I told him about distant times. He interrupted.
> 'I don't think I believe that. Are you a shaman?
> If so where's your reindeer coat. Have another drink.
> If you're a shape-shifter, I'm a truth-teller.
> Drink up, we call it beer, it's strong, it's good.
> You should have been out with us today,
> it isn't every day you catch a mammoth,
> keeps us fed fur a week, fur too, tusks –

> nothing wasted. Spears and arrows both,
> that's what you need, plus a good crowd a boys,
> goo' crowda boys. Take s'moor beer, go on.
> See mamm'ths? Mamm'ths're fuck'n stupit.
> Once they're down they can't get up. Fuck em.
> Y'know this, y'know this, ole shaman-man,
> We'll be here long after mamm'ths're gone.'
>
> He stumbled to his feet, seized a huge torch and ran
> along the wall, making such a wave of sparks
> the painted mammoths kicked and keeled once more.
>
> A deep horn gave this movie-flicker its score. (NSP p 172)

Notice the rhyme in the last two lines. And others: 'man, gone, ran' matching the rhyme-pattern in the first three: 'bard, said, interrupted'. Then – as if incidentally – 'mammoth, both.' Then the internal rhymes: 'truth-teller, beer, stupit, feet'.

All these echoes hold the poem together, while not emphasising rhyme as a main feature. The main feature throughout the poem is voice – natural speech. This voice rhymes spontaneously, as if without being conscious of rhyme in anything like the formal way we might expect of poetry. Rhymes simply cohere in haphazard clusters.

Notice too how the voice gets gradually drunk. What is survival more than a drunken boast? – in Scots at that! Mammoths became extinct through human hunting, yet in these poems nothing seems to have started to go wrong. The sequence hasn't yet reached that far in time. In its beginnings, life seems unstoppable:

> A scum of algae! A greening! A breathing! …
> How far would they go? What would they not try?
> I punched the sky, my friends, I punched the sky. (NSP p 170)

Who is this 'I'? If celebration is his mood and attitude, his stance is that of observer. Like the sequence itself he too can go anywhere. He 'swings in his spacetime hammock,/nibbling a moon or two,' watches dinosaurs, 'they razored through the sultry air', human sacrifice, the Mongols: 'I think they were off to enlarge the known world.' (by conquest) – 'They were like nature, dragons, volcanoes. Keep awake!' After the great flood he gives some advice: 'Build!/ That's what I told them: re-build, but build!' So the pyramids came and he joins the crowds:

> And the bursting wave of music, the brilliant discords,
> the blare, the triumph, the steps of the sound-lords
> bore away like a storm my storyteller's words. (NSP p 174)

The rhythm delivers images, colours, sounds, but above all – movement. With these poems Morgan has a found the voice he always sought. While worlds change about him he stays the same ubiquitous storyteller. Why change from a role which demands no measure of interaction but simply enthusiasm, simply insatiable curiosity? He describes what he sees as if he were the member of an audience watching a film whose sequences flash past like quicksilver, for now it's the world itself which is mercurial, tremendously vivid yet somehow invented, even a little arbitrary, not quite real or demanding. But with the one exception of Copernicus. Here, in the final section of 'Planet Wave', Morgan's admiration is determined, specific, carefully directed. No longer just a storyteller, his tone becomes more weighted, more serious, for with Copernicus the modern world begins.

REFERENCES
CP   *Collected Essays*, 1974, Carcanet, Manchester.
NSP   *New Selected Poems*, 2000, Carcanet, Manchester.
CH   *Chapman Magazine No 64*, Spring/Summer 1991.
GTS   *From Glasgow to Saturn*, 1973, Carcanet, Manchester.

Acts Of Attention: The Poetry of U. A. Fanthorpe

Elizabeth Sandie

One of the first things we need to know when we read a poem is who's speaking the poem. We need to be able to hear its voice or voices and get a sense of who is being addressed. We also need to know what the poem expects of us. Is it allowing us to hear an inner monologue of the poet or a poetic persona? Or is it telling us a story, showing us a scene, a landscape or a dramatic incident, or presenting us with some argument? In any of these scenarios we ask what is it about the way these stories, scenes, thoughts are being voiced that demands our attention. What gives them their significance? Then we need to sort out what is the implication for us as readers of the context and situation created by the poem. How do we engage with its world, respond to its voice?

Recreating Voices

Ursula Fanthorpe is very good at voices. She has the knack of capturing the idiom, dialect and intonation of a wide range of characters, and the voices always come with stage directions, movement, gestures, body language, which are eloquent too. Here for example, the poet and reader are introduced to her cleaner:

> We met in my office door. She'd jammed
> Her hoover in it. *Sorry my lover*, she said
>
> *Don't like to leave it in the passage.*
> *Patients fall over things.* Daily thereafter
>
> She'd hail me; *Still yur then?* And once
> Thassa funny name you got. *Latin Ennit? I'm Olive.*
>
> ['Olive' C:68]

And here, in 'Washing up', she recreates for us her 'doughty mother', her 'magical mother dancing/and singing after the party, under the airer/ With the used tea towels hanging up to dry.' Her snatches of song from opera to popular ballads, sung in a variety of tones from bathos to parody are accommodated within the formal structure of the poem;

> … She liked these ruined maids,
> Or about to be. *No! No! A thousand times no!*
> *You cannot buy my caress. No! No! A thousand times no!*
> *I'd rather die than say yes.* But her feet denied it. [AWB:30/31]

Fanthorpe has created witty monologues for a large cast of fictive characters, some borrowed from other texts, such as the unnamed gentlewoman in 'Macbeth' [ST:53] to the 'Person from Porlock' [VO:72]; other characters are invented: the schoolgirl, for example, no good at the 'terse and cogent' answers demanded by the examiner, who writes to 'Dear Mr. Lee' pouring out her appreciation of *Cider With Rosie* in one long breathless sentence:

> I want to say sorry,
> I didn't want to write a character-sketch
> Of your mother under headings, it seemed
> Wrong somehow when you'd made her so lovely [AWB:22]

In this portrait we see Fanthorpe's sensitivity to that tension in Literature Studies between the affectiveness of the text and a critical appreciation of it. Whatever approaches we adopt, and as this book shows there are lots of them, it is essential to keep the text alive.

Revisiting Roots

Although she assumes many personas and registers in her poetry, gives access to many different voices and discourses which are vividly realised, Fanthorpe also speaks to us in her own voice in a range of tones, at times witty and ironic, at times reflective and elegiac. It's usually an unobtrusive, very English voice. Born in Kent in 1929, she was educated in Oxford and has since spent most of her working life in and around Gloucestershire, firstly teaching, then later 'abandoning responsibility' and becoming 'a middle-aged drop-out' in order to focus her energies on her writing. She is very much 'earthed' in her English landscapes, in 'chalky/Kent mud' and 'serious Cotswold uplands.' ('Earthed' [SE:26]). Like Miranda in *The Tempest* she is 'snared' by 'this narrow island charged with echoes'.

In one of the earliest poems of her first volume, *Side Effects* [1978] Fanthorpe constructed herself as 'A Watcher' [SE:10] of birds and love: 'Not the more common sorts of either kind' but those in rare habitats, including 'the very old, the mad, the failures'.

From her first volume to her latest, *Consequences* [2000] many of her poems invite us to enter her social and geographical landscapes, stand beside her and see with her eyes. What she directs our attention to, are marginal figures and marginal lands. Fanthorpe's poetry is very much about the act of looking, and the relationship of the observer and observed. What makes it special is the nature of the attention she gives to both the inner emotional world and the outer physical, social world. She is fascinated by weather, concerned with the effects of light, literally and metaphorically, on the way the world is seen and represented by artists and writers. Her poems reveal a concern with time, mutability: the way time changes us and the world we live in as well as our ways of seeing and telling.

In voicing these concerns, about who gets into the frame, what is the proper subject of literature, she shares some ground with feminist and marxist critics. Her interest, connected to her birdwatching, in spotting the telling signs, which denote subtle shifts in social attitudes, could be aligned with a school of cultural semiotics. Her awareness that our reading or understanding of incidents, places, texts, relationships, shifts over time is what 'New Historicists' are concerned with. Her attention to the problem of bridging that gap between the world as we experience it, and words adequate to the expression of that experience, is the common concern of poets and linguists. But it is much more interesting to see how her poems can illuminate these theories, than to try to subject the poems to one particular critical approach.

Rethinking Time

Many of Fanthorpe's recurrent themes are evident in 'Stanton Drew'

[SE:28] a poem designed to 'snare' us. It collars us and gives us a set of instructions to help us get to the heart of this place.

> First you dismantle the landscape.
> Take away everything you first
> Thought of. Trees must go,
> Roads, of course, the church,
> Houses, hedges, livestock, a wire
> Fence. The river can stay,
> But loses its stubby fringe
> Of willows. What do you
> See now? Grass, the circling
> Mendip rim, with its notches
> Fresh like carving. A sky
> Like ours, but empty along
> Its lower levels. And earth
> Stripped of its future, tilted
> Into meaning by these stones,
> Pitted and unemphatic. Recreate them.
> They are the most permanent
> Presences here, but cattle, weather,
> Archaeologists have rubbed against them.
> Still in season they will
> Hold the winter sun poised
> Over Maes Knoll's white cheek,
> Chain the moon's footsteps to
> The pattern of their dance.
> Stand inside the circle. Put
> Your hand on stone. Listen
> To the past's long pulse.

There is a presumption, a conceit, that we are standing beside the poet; that 'the landscape' of the first line, which we are being asked to 'dismantle', (and we might not initially understand why we are being asked to do this) is one that we too, can see. In telling us what we have to take away, in order to move back in time, she tells us what is there, now. 'Trees must go,/ Roads, of course, the church,/ Houses, hedges, livestock, a wire/ Fence.' The commas linking this list give us time to visualise these features before they are erased. The 'of course' in that line might be a bit baffling on first reading for those of us who don't know the area, who don't know that 'Stanton Drew' denotes three stone circles on the route south from Bristol towards the Mendip hills. Significantly it's not the famous Stonehenge that demands her attention, but a less well known monument.

We are being asked to function like some kind of Tardis, or time machine. 'The river can stay but loses its stubby fringe/ Of willows.' Then having done the 'dismantling' we're asked to imagine the results. 'What do you/ See now?' Our eye is taken from the foreground, 'Grass,' to a sharp focus on the skyline, 'the circling/ Mendip rim, with its notches/ Fresh, like carving.' After our time travel what we have arrived at is, 'earth/ Stripped of its future, tilted/ Into meaning by these stones,/ Pitted and unemphatic.'

The stones may be 'unemphatic', but the poet is still insistent. 'Recreate them.' All along she is harnessing our imagination to make this poem happen. We are allowed to inch forward again, thinking, in a rather Hardyesque way, of the slow and undramatic effects of time, the way, 'cattle, weather,/ Archaeologists have rubbed against them.' And then the magic happens:

> Still in season they will
> Hold the winter sun poised
> Over Maes Knoll's white cheek,
> Chain the moon's footsteps to
> The pattern of their dance.

On the page the block of verse is monolithic. It is full of stressed, weighty monosyllables, many of them at the beginnings of lines. The image of solidity given by this contrasts now with the feminine curve of the cheek of the hill and the sudden unexpected break into the more tripping rhythm of 'the pattern of their dance.'

Suddenly these stones are alive and sentient, doing the commanding, holding, chaining. The images reveal that illusion of movement, as the light moves round the stones, revealing the secret and the purpose of their location. Those final commands,

> Stand inside the circle. Put
> Your hand on stone. Listen
> To the past's long pulse

if obeyed (and surely they have to be obeyed – those caesuras just before the line ends make us stop and take that mental action – the final three stressed monosyllables enact the very rhythms we are being asked to hear) finally put us right at the centre, not only of the scene we have been asked to envisage and recreate, but of that primal need to connect the human to those forces beyond the earth, to the mysterious powers that control the cycles of sun and moon, that connect us in some spiritual relationship to the natural world we inhabit.

Our ways of telling time have changed, as she points out in one of her many retellings of the Christmas story, 'BC:AD' in *Standing To* [1982:56]. What the 'This' of the opening line is pointing to here is actually the colon between these two abbreviations. Technically speaking, if BC is all of history before Christ and Anno Domini is all those years after, then these two dots in the title stand for the moment when Christ was born. Paradoxically the dots equally signify a moment that couldn't have existed, that in a way isn't counted, doesn't have a date.

> This was the moment when Before
> Turned into After, and the future's
> Uninvented timekeepers presented arms.
>
> This was the moment when nothing
> Happened. Only dull peace
> Sprawled boringly over the earth.
>
> This was the moment when even energetic Romans
> Could find nothing better to do
> Than counting heads in remote provinces.
>
> And this was the moment
> When a few farm workers and three
> Members of an obscure Persian sect
>
> Walked haphazard by starlight straight
> Into the kingdom of heaven.

Our eye takes in the poem as four three-lined stanzas or tercets and a final couplet. We see that the first three of the stanzas set up a pattern, 'This was the moment when …' In the first stanza Fanthorpe imagines this move from BC to AD in terms of a ceremony, a handover, something like the Changing of the Guard. (This imaginative trick of thinking back to a point in the past when our known present is an unknown future, is not unlike what goes on in 'Stanton Drew', though the context is different.)

Some readers have been known to be offended by the second stanza, but we have to hear the ironies here and think about the tone. As well as being playful about the semiotic paradox of that colon, Fanthorpe is reflecting on the way much of recorded history sees wars as 'events' and the bits between, the peace, as non-events, not worth recording. The beginning of the fourth stanza, with that additional 'And', signals what might initially seem only a slight departure from the pattern and a move towards the closure of the poem, as if this is going to be the last definition in the list. It is; but the gap between then end of the tercet and the elision into the final couplet signals a huge departure from the nonchalant, almost deprecatory, tone, to the expansiveness of the complement of the sentence, which acknowledges and weighs the mythic significance of this event against its apparent non-existence.

It is a similar tension between the ordinary and the extraordinary, which informs 'Stanton Drew' and packs that revelatory punch at the end of the poem.

Redefining People

When she turns her attention to people, which she often does, it is to those who would not normally find themselves in the centre of the frame. She explains in an autobiographical essay, 'Slow Learner', that after leaving teaching she took a clerical job in a neurological hospital in Bristol where,

> From my receptionist's glass dugout I watched a world I hadn't imagined, of the epileptic, the depressed, the obsessed, the brain-damaged, the violent, the helpless. I read their case histories written in official medical language, which had its own peculiar effect on me. In these circumstances poetry happened to me. ... if I didn't write about what I saw, nobody would know about it.'   [in Chambers H (ed) *Poetry Matters 5*, Winter 1987]

In this new habitat Fanthorpe became alert to the 'hurly-burly of codes and languages', noticing the huge discrepancy between the talk of the visitors ('lively, affectionate, humane'), the fractured speech of the brain-damaged patients, the 'weasel words' of the doctors and the medical cyphers of the case histories. She became a translator. (See Fanthorpe in Mark and Rees-Jones (eds.) 2000, pp31-4.)

One poem arising from this experience, 'Casehistory: Julie (encephalitis)' [SE:18] captures the distress and disorientation of this patient. The first four lines bring the subject into close focus, not only for the poet, recalling this incident, but for the reader too.

> She stands between us. Her dress
> Is zipped up back to front.
> She has been crying her eyes
> Dark. Her legs are thinner than legs.

The 'us' might have originally been the receptionist and a doctor, or nurse or relative. But this deictic use of pronouns brings us as readers into spatial and psychological proximity with this named patient. The implication is that we, too, can see these details and construe their significance.

These are the only lines of Fanthorpe's in this poem. The rest are 'found' lines; the italicised ones are Shakespeare's and refer to Ophelia's madness. In this new context they interpolate the patient's own voice with its particular idiomatic style and intonation. They serve not only to mark the way her distraught enquiries about her identity fall into discrete, rhythmic stanzas, but also to underline the pathos of her situation. Paradoxically, perhaps, they also allow a little distance, an opportunity to stand back and reflect, place this seering monologue in a literary frame.

> *She is importunate*
>
> I'm not mental am I?
> Someone told me I was mental,
> But I lost me memory
> 'Cos our dad died.
> It don't make sense though, do it?
> After I've been a nurse.
>
> *Her speech is nothing.*

This pattern builds to the final rhetorical, *Do you see this, O God?*

Julie's final question heartbreakingly returns to her starting point,

> What about me dad?
> Me dad's not gone is he?

We see simultaneously the patient's pain in constantly having to meet these griefs afresh, as well as experiencing the uncomfortable, painful immediacy of the listener. The space at the end of the poem implicates us in its silence. What answers can there be to questions such as these?

Vanishing Points

This counterpoint of different registers is one of Fanthorpe's most effective techniques. The nature of different discourses is clarified in these close encounters.

Right from that early poem, 'Watcher', Fanthorpe alerts us to a tension between the speculating eye of the poet trying to appreciate the intrinsic and idiosyncratic qualities of people and places; and the eyes of 'the speculating men', surveying a landscape for its commercial potential, using language to exploit/ develop/ destroy, regardless of those whose habitat it is. This concern reappears in 'A Major Road For Romney Marsh' from the ironically titled *Safe As Houses* [1995]. This is another poem which is structured through contrasting voices and different ways of looking. The poet's voice asserts the special qualities of the area in the opening two lines: 'It is a kingdom, a continent./Nowhere is like it.' Fanthorpe then expands on this in each of the subsequent stanzas to let us see why. This is a lyrical voice by contrast to the offset and parenthesised developer-speak, which interrupts her testimony. But it is rather odd. It holds up for admiration qualities which, in other circumstances, might seem far from laudable, 'truculent churches' 'hermit trees.' Perhaps it is this tenacity in the face of opposition to the elements, 'the windcurled sheep' that is admired; the same tenacity as expressed by 'The Constant Tin Soldier' [ST 86]; qualities that connect the poet to her subject. She talked in interview of her awareness of 'being exposed to extremes' when she was working in the hospital, of having 'to be ready in the same way as a soldier. I think they call it "standing to."' This military metaphor grows out of Fanthorpe's wartime education which she recalls in her article 'War, Poetry and The Child' (Herbert and Hollis (eds.) 2000, pp 208-210).

There is the same sense of readiness here for the fight against the speculators, who, looking on that scene at Romney Marsh see only a site 'ripe for development'. We hear their remorseless litany of what they assume 'it wants' in the offset stanzas ('Kwiksaves,/Artics, Ind Ests, Junctns') but recognize that its present attractiveness lies amongst other things in its *want* or lack of these features. The poet's final assertion, 'It is itself and different', stands on its own to give us time to weigh that evidence and see this *ought* to be sufficient justification in itself to demand protection. At the same moment of recognising that statement's power, we see its impotence in the face of the inexorable march of so-called progress. The line is capped by the reductive yet plangent '(Nt fr lng. Nt fr lng)'. In order to voice this line we have resist this disintegration of language and reinstate the vowels. This poem achieves its full impact in that tension between its spoken and written form.

This sense of loss, or impending loss, of ways of life permeates Fanthorpe's work. We hear it in her later poem, 'Widening the Westway' [C:50]. As the JCBs move in for the final stages of a 'protracted ending' for 'an avenue full of confident thirties semis,' Fanthorpe observes the houses opposite 'watching speechless'. 'Atrocity/ is what we haven't got used to yet'. The 'yet' is ominous and in her most recent poems she looks at an England in which the choices for the future seem to be reduced to theme park or business centre.

England – Myths and Realities

A more lighthearted use of contrasting voices can be found in Fanthorpe's poem, 'Not My Best Side' [1978:38] in which she rereads Ucello's picture 'Saint George and the Dragon' (reproduced on the front of her first volume *Side Effects*) giving a contemporary voice to the dragon, the monster and the girl. She's not sure if she wants to be rescued, finds the dragon:

So nicely physical, with his claws
And lovely green skin, and that sexy tail.

While the egotistical Saint George, with his 'diplomas in Dragon/
Management and Virgin Reclamation' asks:

Don't
You want to carry out the roles
That sociology and myth have designed for you?

the girl doesn't get the chance to bellow NO! The hero doesn't bother
to wait for an answer, sweeps her needs to one side, ends this trilogy
of monologues with,

What, in any case does it matter what
You want? You're in my way.

The poem helps us see Ucello's painting afresh. Our eye is directed
to details we might have overlooked; to aspects of the structure, and
rhythm of the composition, to its narrative; to its *ways* of telling, to
the pictorial conventions of Ucello's day. This picture is part of the
National Gallery's recent exhibition 'Telling Time.' As the reviewer
Laura Cumming points out:

> The picture compresses a day of action in one spectacular still
> … George arrives on his bucking charger, the tip of his lance
> piercing the furious dragon, which has already been roped by
> the princess who will eventually lead it, vanquished, back to
> the town it has been terrorising. The narrative runs seamlessly
> through the line-up, left to right, from the horse's flying tail to
> the royal hem progressing out of the picture. (*The Observer*
> October 15, 2000)

The tripartite structure of the poem echoes the painter's 'obsession
with/ Triangles.' Just as there is a line which takes the eye through
the painting, so there are connecting threads, which link the three
sections of the poem and make us look and look again at various
elements of the composition.

We are enabled to see the crucial difference a shifting perspective
makes, whether these are perspectives of time, or gender, or status, to
the way a subject is narrated. What the monster sees in derogatory
terms as 'A horse with the deformed neck and square hoofs' is seen

by its owner as 'the latest model, with/ Automatic transmission and built-in obsolescence'. In re-viewing this picture and retelling its story in a modern idiom, Fanthorpe is being very entertaining, yet at the same time she presents an incisive image of contemporary society, its jargons, its changing sexual morality and fashions, its goal-oriented consumerism, its emphasis on self image, its self-seeking.

We can follow this poem in two directions. It's interesting to compare its reflections on contemporary society with a poem two decades on, which in a post-Thatcherite, New Labour era, seems to have a much sharper edge to its satire. 'Autumn Offer' [C:72] announces:

> Vacancies available now
> For the next millennium's consumers, investors,
> And personnel. We supply
> State-of-the-art instruction – the leaner, fitter curriculum
> …
> We have axed from our course modules that clearly
> Have long passed their sell-by-date:
> Art, music, history, literature, religion.

'The leaner, fitter curriculum' belongs to the same breed of word mongering as 'surgical strike,' implying a beneficial intent for an action which is in fact deadly.

That parodic echo of Keats' 'Ode to Autumn', with its lyrical 'Season of mists' which inscribed such a sense of imminent loss, laces together these stanzas, full of management speak.

(Season of texts, and learning what to think…)

This technique, so typical of Fanthorpe, of syncopating two different registers, is powerful enough to make us recognise and resist the current educational ideology, which insists:

> Our youngsters must learn to grow up
> Aggressive, acquisitive, mean.

Close Looking

The world portrayed in Sir Luke Fildes' painting which appears on the front cover of *A Watching Brief* [1987] and which Fanthorpe addresses in her poem also entitled 'The Doctor', has its cruelties and heartaches too, but in many senses it shows a more benign world. This is the second direction from 'Not My Best Side' – to look at other poems responding to paintings. (This one can be found in the Tate Gallery's anthology, edited by Peter Adams (1993) *With A Poet's Eye*.) 'The Doctor' draws our attention to this Victorian narrative painting, via the two contemporary attendants who stand either side of it looking like subjects someone is about to paint. Their conversations about contemporary ways of death, pneumonia in old age, frame the poem. Their scepticism about modern doctors' ability to 'really know' the condition of the heart is contrasted, firstly with the surrounding painters' examination and intuitive knowledge of the immanence of death, and secondly, their scepticism contrasts with the certainties of the Victorian Doctor:

> Who has done all he can, and knows nothing
> Will help or heal, sits raptly, raptly,
> As if such absorbed attention were in itself
> A virtue. As it is.

While the light in the painting focuses our attention on the child centre stage who 'frets in its fever', Fanthorpe moves, via the parents who 'grieve in the background gloom' to examine the doctor, the quality of the 'absorbed attention' he is paying to the small dying child. [1987:10] Not only the painter and the Doctor, but the poet too belongs to those 'patient watchers' who 'have eyes for those who watch'.

That quality of absorbed attention is a quality Fanthorpe appreciates in the *Journals of Dorothy Wordsworth*. In 'Deer in Gowbarrow Park' [AWB:14] Fanthorpe rereads Dorothy's journal entry for April 15, 1802. This records the experience, shared with her brother William, which gave rise to his poem 'Daffodils'. Despite his reliance on her notes, she has been erased from the scene in his version of that day. Fanthorpe savours the 'straggle of unplanned delights and scrambles,/ Texture of wind and wetness, glancing/ Touch of the day' that the journal provides and notices some of the especially vivid detail in Dorothy's account, which William didn't work into his poem: 'the daffodils *about the breadth/ of a country turnpike road* ... and *N.B. Deer/ In Gowbarrow Park like skeletons*'. Fanthorpe recognises that this is too striking and disturbing an image to have any place in the 'tame' poem of William's. Images such as these 'defy the taming mind'.

Dorothy certainly wasn't a tame person. De Quincey, another famous writer of that period said, 'She was all fire and ardour ... this ardour looked out in every gleam of her wild eyes'. [De Quincey 1970:188] Coleridge saw Dorothy as William's 'exquisite sister' and considered her

> a Woman of Genius ... and but for the absorption of her whole Soul in her Brother's fame and writings would, perhaps in a different style have been as great a Poet as himself. [letter to Anne Scott 26 Aug 1833: *Collected Letters vol VI* Letter 1788]

When I was a student Dorothy's journals were seen by many to be of interest only in so far as they cast light on William's creative processes. Now her writing is studied for its own sake too. (See the Appendix at the end of this essay for further details.)

Fanthorpe's additional NB at the end of the poem is drawing attention to the way Dorothy can single out such vivid details to 'hands us that day'. With an equally sharp eye, Fanthorpe is also adept at accumulating detail to give us the full texture of apparently ordinary events such as 'Chaplaincy Fell Walk' [VO:66], and 'Queuing Outside the Jeu de Paume in Light Rain' [AWB:36]. These are both charged with a sense of absence, addressed in fact to an absent partner.

This is how it is here

What Dorothy did for daffodils, Fanthorpe does for bluebells in 'Conygre Wood and Hyakinthoides Non-Scriptus' [C:39], a title which seems cumbersome with its mouthful of a complicated sounding Latin tag. This in fact denotes the native English bluebell, the unmarked, 'non-scriptus' version which thrives in the wild, in woodlands, as opposed to the 'Hyakinthoides hispanicus', the cultivated Spanish version, 'the best garden bluebell, bigger, easier to grow, which soon forms large majestic clumps' (according to Reader's Digest: *A Garden For All Seasons*). If you try to look up bluebell in the index here, you will get redirected to Endymion, an alternative classification for our native bluebell.

In the first stanza, Fanthorpe presents us with notes that could have come from an artist's sketchbook, with sound track attached.

> This is how it is, here:
> Native halflight. Rain off the Atlantic.
> Rack of blue like sky growing
> a foot above ground. Hush. Birdcalls.
> Small puckered beech leaves, and earth,
> Its muscles showing, hurdling up limestone,
> With acres of blue on its back.

As we move from that deliberately unwieldy title to the first line of simple English monosyllables, 'This is how it is here', we become immediately aware of the incongruity, that wide gap of registers, a dichotomy which tensions the whole poem. Fanthorpe is a writer well versed in history, who frequently alludes to myths, as she does in the second stanza here, who like all good writers is interested in the etymology of words and the rich connotations they bring with them. She is equally aware, that 'Words as plain as hen birds wings,/ Do not lie, /Do not overbroider things'. [Larkin 1988:26]

The 'This' of that first line leads us not only to a description of a very specific bluebell wood on a specific day, but also into a rumination about Englishness. She shows that a lot of its real pleasures are the unmarked, unnamed, unsung, apparently ordinary things, which in fact can be extraordinarily wonderful. I wonder if the poem was written in the spring of 2000, a particularly spectacular year for bluebells. A phenomenon which I witnessed not in Conygre wood, but here in North Yorkshire, in other secret and magical places, in Hackfall Woods above Greweltorpe, and in Sleightholme Dale. (Don't whatever you do tell the developers about them.)

Her argument in the second stanza counters the 'Dons, doctors, name-givers' who see this species as nondescript. Only if we accept their view can it be denigrated as 'this lot' and inferior. In the reiteration of its colour: 'Blue and blue and blue', she lets us see the density and extent of its blueness, much, much greater we imagine than even the width of a turnpike road. She celebrates this flower, withholding its common name till the final line of the poem where it resonates with the full weight of her description.

Poetry Lesson

It was Seamus Heaney who said that 'the art of being a poet lies in the summoning of the energies of words.' [Heaney 1980:36] In this poem Fanthorpe is comparing the energies of some of the simplest of English words with their Latin counterparts. In this instance she doesn't want to be encumbered by the associations with the story of Endymion, the 'invented grief'. She wants to see things afresh. Fanthorpe defined one of her main concern as a desire 'to find out and put down faithfully what it is that is trying to get itself said'. [Wainwright 1995:74] While a head full of literary, biblical and mythical allusions can be a storehouse of ideas and an advantage to a poet, there are times when literary precedents can get in the way.

This is a problem she confronts in the opening line of 'Another Swan Poem'. [C:66]

(Again it's rather an odd title. It's almost telling you not to bother with it, as in 'just another', as if they're ten a penny.) 'This Swan knows too much poetry' it begins, grabbing our attention with this obvious fallacy.

> *Another Swan Poem*
>
> This swan knows too much poetry.
> It came knocking at the window
>
> Importunate, drumming Tap-Tap
> Like a midnight lover. This is
>
> Early morning for us, Swan. It
> Takes not a blind bit of. It stands

On water, wings spreadeagling,
Neck rampant, mouthing *Me. You. Now.*

Eat. Now. You. Me. No magic shirt,
No ducal coronet, just bare

Swan, mouthing *Me. Eat. You.* Nervous,
We fetch the brown sliced. The snake-neck

Lunges as we cast Hovis on
The water. Vindictively it

Dunks, drowns, swallows. Rears up again.
Romance is what it wants. Savage

Black eyes peer close. We can number
The brownish forehead feathers. Far

Too near. The long beak opens, long
And oval-ended, containing

A sharp active tongue. The creature
Seeks to be seductive. Wants us

To slot our bread inside its beak.
We do it, gingerly, trying

Not to touch. It accepts the slice,
Dips it, comes back, until the last

Scatter of crumbs. Reluctantly
It navigates away. A faint

Me. You. comes sighing down the water.

This is not a good poem about a swan,
But it might be the bravest. It is also true.

While the actual swan doesn't know any poetry at all, the *image* of the swan in her head that's trying to get written, is competing with other inscriptions of swanness that are already stored there, not least of which will be Yeats' poems 'The Wild Swans At Coole' and 'Leda and the Swan'. Were these in her mind too when writing 'Found on the Battlefield', the opening poem of *Consequences* where she sees 'Swans cruise, freighted with meaning,/ Eloquent and ferocious as heraldry'? This swan is going to be different. We hear how:

It came knocking at the window

Importunate, drumming Tap-tap
Like a midnight lover

In doing so it brings with it recollections, not only of other swans but of Ted Hughes' 'Thought Fox'. This is also a poem about the problems of writing a poem. Many of the words and images are deliberately domestic; the reference to 'the hovis', the 'dunking', 'the last scatter of crumbs', trying to keep this swan out of that emblematic field, but it is nonetheless alluded to, at times through negatives, 'No magic shirt, /No ducal coronet'. But what 'rears up again' from time to time, despite the poet's best intentions, are those swan-like features that leant themselves to the myth makers in the first place, the 'wings spreadeagling', the neck 'rampant'. Its seductiveness, its desire for romance are hard to eradicate.

This swan is subjected to an ornithologist's scrutiny:

we can number
The brownish forehead feathers. Far

Too near. The long beak opens, long
And oval-ended, containing

A sharp active tongue.

What's made equally vivid to us is the wonderful sound the swan makes as it approaches and recedes, and the way the observers read these sounds shows their sense that it has them in its sights, has intentions, not quite as rapacious as in Yeats, but nonetheless … 'Me. You. Now./Eat. Now. You. Me.'

Fanthorpe has said that if she has any objective it is 'to bear witness, to say, "I have seen this, and no one else was there looking at that precise moment." In order to write I have to concentrate, and concentration is a form of love.'

One scene that she witnessed was a rather unusual poetry lesson which she recreates for us in 'Seminar: Felicity and Mr Frost' [VO:60]:

Two truth-tellers are here;
Marigold-headed Felicity (three)
Has come because of the hole in the roof.

> Mr Frost, who is dead, comes in black
> On white. He has something to tell us.

Fanthorpe focuses on the young child's difficulties in understanding the conversations she's overhearing. If we were having a seminar now, someone might ask, who's this Mr. Frost in the first verse?' Others might have come across the American poet Robert Frost and recognise the reference to his poems 'Mending Wall' and 'Stopping by Woods on a Snowy Evening'. [p 33 & 145 of the Penguin Poets edition] Perhaps he has been given the courtesy title 'Mr.' by the child?

> *I didn't understand the story*
> *The man was telling us* she says clearly
> Underneath the table the table. Mr Frost
> Sticks to his story, but his voice is opaque.

The poet imagines Felicity's struggle to relate the now of the poem to the now of the seminar room.

> Mr Frost's world is secret too.
> There are woods in it, and miles to go,
>
> And snow. It has started to rain
> Where we are. Felicity stands on a chair
> To look out. *Don't ever have children,*
> Her mother smiles at the students.
>
> And miles to go. *You said*
> *Don't have children* (Felicity cancels
> Her secret world). The students are concerned.
> It is still raining. Her mother translates:
>
> *I didn't mean it.* And snowing.
> Mr Frost is preoccupied. He
> Has promises to keep. And miles to go.

You might like to look at Frost's poem and think what observations and questions the students would have raised in the seminar. It is a poem that creates a sense of mystery and deliberately withholds a lot of information. Like the wall, it has lots of gaps in it. Perhaps the evocation of this still moment in the wood has its impact because we don't know who the traveller is, or where he's going or why.

The attention in Fanthorpe's poem shifts from trying to fathom

'Mr Frost', to trying to make sense of the mother's utterance. The poet is aware simultaneously of its different significance to Felicity; to the students; to the mother. The poet alerts us to those huge problems of how words mean and don't mean what they say. It shows that words are acts, can change things, have significance, are hard to cancel; but it also shows the complexities of the meaning-making process, the complex cultural contexts in which they live.

In any reading encounter the reader brings to the text their own experience of the world and their own experience of how texts go. It therefore follows that the answers to those questions raised in the introduction will change across time, and that they will differ from those of fellow readers who come to the poems from different social, educational and cultural contexts.

At times Fanthorpe can herself be a very resistant reader, as in 'Knowing about Sonnets: Lesson 1: *The Soldier* (Brooke)' [VO:57] She explains on the tape *Double Act* that this was written in response to a lecture she was allowed to watch when she was a writer in residence at St. Martin's, Lancaster. The subject of the lecture was sonnets and the example Rupert Brooke's 'The Soldier'. The epigraph to her poem is taken from Terry Eagleton's *Criticism and Ideology*

Fanthorpe was aware she says, of two voices, the lecturer's telling the students how to control sonnets, and the poet's trying to face the thought that, though he was young and gifted, he might be going to die quite soon. 'Oddly,' she says, 'the lecturer didn't seem to notice what the poet was saying.'

In the poem that follows Fanthorpe playfully deconstructs this deconstructive approach, while letting us hear the full resonance of Brooke's opening hypothesis 'If I should die'. In performance Rosie Bailey plays the lecturer/critic's voice while Ursula Fanthorpe, in a hushed but increasingly urgent tone, struggles to be allowed to articulate Brooke's opening line. Their intonation creates a very dramatic tension between the competing and insistent 'Think This' of the poet and critic. The squeezing of the gap between reminds us how little time or space is given for the affectiveness of poetry, which is all too often forgotten in competing schools of critical theoreticians.

Reflections

It would be easy to subject Fanthorpe's poetry to critical scrutiny from a range of positions, from feminist to formalist. A single critical perspective would be reductive, and inappropriate for a poet whose writings warn above all against the rampant reductiveness of our culture. Unlike the lecturer in 'Knowing About Sonnets' in a line ironically appropriated from Brooke, I don't want to say, 'Think this, think only this.'

What I want to be allowed to do, and want my students to do, is to give the same 'absorbed attention' to her poems as she gives to her subjects. I want to acknowledge that her writings, like those of Dorothy Wordsworth whom she so much admires, can 'hand us that day', give us the quiddity, the 'thisness' of her lived experience, so that we hear things afresh, see them in a new light.

To find a way into any poem it is important to be aware of the way the poet, 'summons the energies of words', to be alert to the rhythms of the poem's images and ideas, to be attentive to its voices, to feel its pulse.

I want the poet's voice to be louder than the critic's.

As Fanthorpe says in ' Of Mutability',

> ...the finite scenes
> Of birth and death recur. But things done,
> Meals cooked, fires lit, trees planted, words said,
> Poems observed, have their own posterity. [AWB:63]

I can only add N.B. N.B.

REFERENCES
U. A. Fanthorpe is published by Peterloo Poets, The Old Chapel, Calstock, Cornwall: *Side Effects* (1978), *Standing To* (1982), *Voices Off* (1984), *A Watching Brief* (1987), *Neck Verse* (1992), *Safe As Houses* (1995), *Consequences* (2000).
Her *Selected Poems* were published in 1986: Peterloo hb. King Penguin pb.
Audio cassettes   *Awkward Subject* (Peterloo); *Double Act* (Penguin)
Fanthorpe talks about writing *Consequences* in *PBS Bulletin* Summer 2000 (p14). It is reviewed by Hubert Moore in *The North 27* Winter 2000 (p40)
Eddie Wainwright, *Taking Stock: A First Study of The Poetry of U. A. Fanthorpe*, U.A. Fanthorpe 'Hospital Speak: The Neuro-psychiatric Unit' in Alison Mark

and Deryn Rees-Jones (eds.) 2000 *Contemporary Women's Poetry: Reading/ Writing/Practice* (Macmillan)
U.A. Fanthorpe 'War, Poetry and The Child' in W.N. Herbert and M.Hollis (eds.) 2000 *Strong Words: Modern Poets on Modern Poetry* (Bloodaxe) Peterloo (1995). (This includes Fanthorpe's article 'Slow Learner'.)
Seamus Heaney, *Preoccupations* (1980)
Philip Larkin, *The Collected Poems* (1988)
Thomas De Quincey, *Recollections of the Lakes and Lake Poets*, Penguin (1970)

APPENDIX: Dorothy Wordsworth

For more of Dorothy's Journals see Mary Moorman's *Journals of Dorothy Wordsworth* (2nd edition), Oxford (1980).Many of the entries show a similar interest in weather and the effects of light, see for example:

> As I sat down on the grass I observed the glittering silver line on the ridges of the backs of the sheep, owing to their situation respecting the sun – which made them look beautiful but with some strangeness, like animals of another kind, as if belonging to a more splendid world. [Moorman ed. p117-8. 29/4/1802]

> The night was wild. There was a strange Mountain lightness when we were at the top of White Moss. I have observed it there in the evenings between the two valleys. There is more of the sky there than in any other place … [p.86. 8/1802]

> Helm Crag was distinct. The dead hedge round Benson's field bound together at the top by an interlacing of ash sticks which made a chain of silver when we faced the moon [p112. 17/4/02]

> We walked round Rydal lake – rich, calm, streaked, very beautiful.

> A very fine moonlight night – the moon shone like herrings in the water. [p.49 31/10/1800]

A.G.Hill summarises the impression we get of Dorothy's daily life from her letters and journals. It consists of,

> Reading, conversing with poets and writers and neighbours and passing vagrants above all walking, and baking and making giblet pies and washing the linen and gathering mosses, rowing over to spend an evening with friends playing cards , taking tea and walking and writing for William and cleaning and papering and making shoes and clothes and having an occasional stab at writing poetry and thinking she can't do it, writing letters , entertaining visitors , looking after everybody else's children travelling. [Hill A.G. (ed) 1981 *Letters Of Dorothy Wordsworth* p46.]

It is insights such as these that gave rise to Lynn Peters' poem 'Why Dorothy Wordsworth Is Not As Famous As Her Brother', which appears together with William's 'Daffodils' and the relevant extract from Dorothy's journal in Rob

Pope's *The English Studies Book,* p 338-340

There is a good study of Dorothy Wordsworth by R. Gittings and J. Manton, Oxford 1985. They comment of the earlier Alfoxton Journal:

> entries are practically in note form. Nothing distracts. The acute observation by Dorothy is there, but no Dorothy herself. Every object, sight, sound is allowed its own nature. A warm day is built from a series of impressions, matter of fact but cumulative. [77]

Some reviewers and critics see Fanthorpe as being equally self-effacing; look at her poem 'Awkward subject' where she feels uncomfortable at the need to have her photograph taken to publicise her book. Photograph the poems, not me, she says.

See also:
Virginia Woolf's portrait 'Dorothy Wordsworth' in *The Common Reader* (2nd series)
De Quincey, T., *Recollections of the Lakes and Lake Poets*, Penguin 1970
Gunn E., 1981 *A Passion for the Particular*, Gollanz.
Simons Judy, 1990 *Diaries and Journals of Literary Women from Fanny Burney to Virginia Woolf*, Macmillan
Homans M., 1980, *Women Writers and Poetic Identity*: Princetown U.P. New Jersey

'The Jewel You Lost': Birthday Letters, Ted Hughes

Paul Mills

Writers, readers and teachers

Making notes while re-reading *Birthday Letters* I drew on a blank A4 sheet of paper a cone: circle up, point down. The poems themselves make frequent reference to symbols, structures and shapes, but this particular structure does not appear anywhere in the book, so why a cone? I drew it because, reading through it again, the whole collection seemed to me cone-like. If the circle at the top represents breadth – a wide engagement with many kinds of experience – the point at the foot of the cone has another logic. The progression of *Birthday Letters* is a spiralling down towards the point at its base.

Almost all poets whose work receives critical attention at the moment stay with the circle, and there's much sense in that. Their aim is to travel widely through experience. Only there can they hope to reveal with sufficient scope the various threads which make contemporary reality. But *Birthday Letters,* Ted Hughes' final collection of poems, lowers us precariously into the cone, tightens the circle. At its point is the death of his first wife, Sylvia Plath. Its ultimate shape is focused on her drive towards suicide. The whole book is a cone and centrifugal. One might even argue that every poem spirals down from a wide field towards that death at the centre.

In my own dealings with this book I am setting out to consider the implications, and the procedures, which the writing of *Birthday Letters* highlights. Just as we thought we might have got rid of judgements that sifted poets of major significance from a vast, jostling plethora of others, a book arrives that seems to retrigger in us the need to recognise something beyond the usual order. What should we say? What do we want? What might this book help us to understand?

Some of us writing these chapters are poets ourselves. Some are also involved in teaching writing. Many of our readers will be students of creative writing or in the process of learning how to read contemporary poetry. Are these activities perhaps similar? Teaching, writing, reading – whether we are engaged in one or in all of these things, has *Birthday Letters* something to tell us? What kind of light, or shadow, does it cast? Can we all, whatever we do, learn something from it? Since it records the story of two very significant writers, does it have things to say which we need to hear?

As a poet and teacher of creative writing, at some point I ask my students to redeem from memory places, things, experiences or events which have become lodged in their imagination. Some things will have been stored at the back of their minds – something in childhood, something which might have happened only a week, a day, or even just hours before. There will be things that aren't just memory but which will have acquired a particular colour, an unusual resonance. Ordinary memory will have transferred certain impressions into imagination, and these will be part of ourselves as individuals, also of who we are as a culture. We might not know why these things are transferred, or why certain events feel so different. Knowing why isn't really the business. Writing about them, and making them real, is, however, and if attention is given to the imagination in this way, the idea is that it will collect more and more experiences, more and more significance will be available. The idea behind this method is a belief – that imagination acts as a shaping force, is more intelligent than our ordinary minds. Imagination is present in each one of us. It is what defines us as a species. To write, paint, or do whatever imagination offers, requires a kind of listening to its suggestions.

In creative writing workshops the role of the imagination can of course be supplied by other means. The imagination itself can say to the writer 'Write about this. Write in this way or that.' One feels prompted to write about certain subjects and not others. But in practice the tutor can just as usefully act as a prompt, so that students are invited to listen to his or her directives. The ideas is that prompting comes, or seems to come, from elsewhere. There is nothing sinister or arcane about this process of relating to something (or someone) delivering directions from outside. No one needs to be conjuring with the malevolent supernatural, but simply investigating how meaning is made – through images, sounds, voices, words and ideas. For a new generation of writers and readers, suicide is not the ceremony at which they all hope to graduate. Hughes himself in this book speaks for the living, for survival. Imagination does not necessarily point down to a point of no return, as it seemed to have done for Sylvia Plath. In contrast it can point to a widening out, a wider state of sympathy and enrichment.

An increased sympathy for Sylvia Plath may indeed be one of the aims and conclusions of *Birthday Letters*, in the sense that we gain more understanding about her experiences. But this sympathetic widening does not seem to have been her own directive as a poet. Instead, her attention came to be focused more and more exclusively on her dead father. Otto Plath died when Sylvia was eight. In *Ariel* (1965), written during her final months, she became obsessed with the power of death over life, and gradually surrendered herself to it. In 'The Table' (BL 138) Hughes describes how he made her a desk using 'coffin timber. Coffin elm' yet without any foredoomed feeling or hint in his mind that he was prescribing the poems she would write there. 'I did not / Know I had made and fitted a door / Opening downward into your Daddy's grave.'

At points Hughes confesses his role as tutor: 'Finding your father for you and then / Leaving you to him.' At the same time he acts as her nurse or comforter, reacting with horror to the directives his wife was beginning to receive from this new source. Otto became her tutor from then on. Inspiration welled up from her dreams:

> Your day-waking was a harrowed safety
> You tried to cling to – not knowing
> What had frightened you
> Or where your poetry followed you from
> With its blood-sticky feet. Each night
> I hypnotised calm into you,
> Courage, understanding, and calm.

> Did it help? Each night you descended again
> Into the temple-crypt.
> That private, primal cave
> Under the public dome of father-worship.
> All night you lolled unconscious
> Over the crevasse   ('Dream Life', BL 141)

The position Hughes dramatises here – Plath as the bride-priestess of her dead father – is not one he adopts towards her. She does not become a goddess for him like Otto was a god for her. Her death does not trap him into a posthumous search. Instead he becomes Plath's dramatist-storyteller.

Characters

This shifting of roles – husband-tutor, husband-nurse – grows increasingly urgent for Hughes towards the end of the story. We get the sense that he no longer knew how to react or who he should be. He could not become 'storyteller' until the story had run its inevitable course. That it was inevitable, or that it seemed so retrospectively, accounts for the artistic treatment of characters in the story. Clearly those we are bound to be most concerned with are 'I' and 'You', the two poets Hughes and Plath. But since a force of dramatic inevitability guides the events, these characters function in the story like puppets, both helpless. They are strung, dragged, prompted, and forced to play their various parts by 'it' – one of the book's most commonly occurring words – as in the 'it' of 'Your Paris', '... it sealed/The underground, your hide-out,/That chamber, where you still hung waiting/For your torturer.' Or in 'Moonwalk' – '... it flings/On to the X-ray plate the shape of the ape/Being led by the virgin, both helpless/In her hell', so that neither seem responsible for the world they inhabit or create: 'Bosch/Held out a spidery hand and you took it/Timidly, a bobby-sox American./You saw right down to the Goya funeral grin/and recognised it/and recoiled ...' Nor are they able to escape it. 'It' might be 'Bosch' here (with its slang echo for 'Germans'). In other poems 'it' is a daemon, the Ogre, the Moon, Daddy, Ouija, Spain, a bullet, fever or panic. But ultimately 'it' is the story, the god, the myth. 'You could not explain it .../ "God is speaking through me," you told me./"Don't say that," I cried. "Don't say that./That is horribly unlucky."' ('The God' BL 191).

The characters belong to worlds of the inevitable, hence the recurring emphasis given to star-signs, omens, astrology: 'That day the solar system married us/Whether we knew it or not,' hence too the strong impression of characters with comparatively small parts to play being quickly discarded from the drama. The crowded whirl of Cambridge and London life served its purpose, but only as the circumference of the circle from which Hughes and Plath would start to make their increasingly focused descent, focused initially on each other. And focus itself, the sharpness of realisation it brought their poems, worked on each of them in their early relationship:

> First sight. First snapshot isolated
> Unalterable, stilled in the camera's glare.
> Taller
> Than ever you were again. Swaying so slender
> It seemed your long, perfect, American legs
> Simply went on up. That flaring hand.
> Those long, balletic, monkey-elegant fingers.
> And the face – a tight ball of joy.
> I see you there, clearer, more real
> Than in any of the years in its shadow –
> As if I saw you that once, then never again.
> The loose fall of hair – that floppy curtain
> Over your face, over your scar. And your face
> A rubbery ball of joy
> Round the African-lipped, laughing, thickly
> Crimson-painted mouth. And your eyes
> Squeezed in your face, a crush of diamonds,
> Incredibly bright, bright as a crush of tears
> That might have been tears of joy, a squeeze of joy.
> ('St Botolph's' BL 15)

In this passage, Hughes the lover and Hughes the poet are one. The youthful lover and mature poet are the same in their depth of focused seeing. Hughes was to find his subjects for poems simply through that 'once, then never again' kind of attention – to pike, thrushes, landscapes, actions, events. Whether the poet was to learn from the lover how this is done, or the other way round, it was to become his most recognisable trait, almost his signature: the trained eye, words getting all their clues from the eye in a single glimpse. It is no accident that eyes are the subject here, the words trying to feel their way towards them, around them, as if his fingertips were possessed of sight, keen to miss nothing, every piece of verbal equipment engaged. The words might seem to fall out almost at random, but with an increasing sense being savoured. As the passage moves to its close in the last four lines, 'squeeze, crush, tears, joy, bright' keep recurring, find new positions, just as 'ball, face, joy' had done earlier. And these words were surely selected out for their active quality: 'squeeze, crush', while the other significant words: 'eyes, diamonds, tears, joy,' achieve force by their place at the ends of lines.

It follows however that not every character in the story will be receiving maximum focus attention. Lucas is just Lucas, 'my friend, one/Among those three or four who stay unchanged'. And Hughes himself? '[I didn't know] I was being auditioned/For the male lead in your drama.' In its later stages few characters remain, Sylvia's mother Aurelia ('Your mother/Played Prospero, flying her magic in/To stage the masque') and of course her father, Hughes and Plath themselves and their two children, Frieda (aged two) and Nick their second child. The birth of the children interrupted the drama. The vortex for a period stopped its descent:

> It was not Death
> Weeping in you then, when you lay among bloody cloths
> Holding what had come out of you to cry. ('Isis', BL 112)

The American poet Marianne Moore appears, to be dismissed. ('Her lips put me in mind of a child's purse/Made of the skin of a dormouse'), in 'The Literary Life', but far more significant to Hughes was another old woman, a gypsy beggar whose request for money outside the cathedral in Rheims Plath had dismissed. This French gypsy turned out to be not quite so irrelevant however:

> Like a pistol her finger
> Came up to your face, all her momentum
> Icicled into a pointer: 'Vous

Creverez bientot.' Her dark face
A knot of oiled leather, a quipu.
Like Geronimo's. Bitter eyes
Of grappa-dreg revenge, old Gallic malice.
          ('The Gypsy' BL 117)

In an instant this old woman foresees Sylvia's future. Was this a prediction? or a curse? To Hughes in retrospect, and to his readers, the gypsy's words ('You will die soon') were to become momentous. As the poem makes clear he took them seriously even on that day in the street in Rheims – as if he half-recognised their accuracy, either because of his own concealed anxieties about Sylvia, or, more likely, out of respect for the power of intuitive perception, recognising its source. 'Heavier than the Cathedral' and 'like a newer or much older religion' the curse had life, power, ancient authority, and could be lifted, if at all, only by equal and parallel sets of magical operations, only by forms of sympathetic ritual or poetry. So he watches the gypsy going her way among the café tables, among the tourists, confessing – too late – how he wanted to call her back, give her some money – just a coin might do it. He sees himself afterwards trying to remove the curse by less secure methods. 'For days I rhymed / Talismans of power, in cynghanedd / to neutralise her venom.' In the rest of the poem he describes his attempts in a mood of self-mocking commentary. Whether he believed or half-believed in affective magic or ritual intervention, no such protective object ('Talisman') or language instructed by early Celtic poetry ('cynghanedd') sufficed. Regular in its use of internal rhyme and alliteration, cynghanedd influenced English poetry through Hopkins, later through Hughes himself. Despite his playful reference to it here, it signifies his rootedness and commitment – not just to a poetic style but also towards certain gifts of perception. What survives in our own impression of this encounter however is its seriousness, and the poem makes sure this impression holds.

But what is 'The Gypsy' saying to us in terms of the narrative sequence of *Birthday Letters*? Are these poems merely anecdotal? They go further than anecdote, bringing into concentrated form what would otherwise stay as just pervasive but diffuse feeling. 'The Gypsy' is no exception. The face that gives him pause here (and a very different face from Sylvia's) evokes poetic resources different again. These are Hughes' own and oppose hers; they belong to Elmet, the Celts, to an earlier pre-Roman, pre-Christian Europe, with links to the Native Americans (Geronimo). To Hughes the old woman's face has a tribal function, mask-like, therefore with practical consequences. Also by this logic it's a 'quipu' – a corded knot used in ancient Peru for keeping accounts. And doubtless for him the accounts she keeps are deadly in this case. His trained eye finds this face exactly – 'oiled leather'. Yet what did this incident mean to Plath? His mood records strong hints of annoyance. The curse in his view has happened to them both. 'But you / Never mentioned it. Never recorded it / In your diary.' He hopes she somehow maybe didn't hear it, too immersed to pay it any attention – 'Deafened, maybe, / By closer explosions. Closed, maybe, / In a solider crypt.' The poem ends here with the word 'crypt', implying that to Hughes in retrospect this was a deeply ominous immersion, signalling in itself what was to come.

To Plath the incident hadn't happened. It was as if the gypsy wasn't there. In one obvious sense this was a mercy; in another the event foretold not only her future but the growing conflict within their marriage. Not only has she not heard, she has not *seen* – her eye has not been trained for this encounter, nor has her training as a poet alerted her to the gypsy's present and resonant actuality, her Power. Inscribed in the poem is Plath's dismissal not just of the gypsy but of Hughes' own inspirational sources, his Power, drawn from his knowledge of totem tribal culture and its narratives. His imaginative fascination with Plath's face earlier brought him to notice her 'African-lipped' mouth. Africa, Native America, Spain: to Plath these were triggers of fear and resistance. But here she hasn't noticed, hasn't even recorded it in her diary. The gypsy has been several times ignored. Hughes is trapped between trying to protect his wife, and sharing the gypsy's sense of exclusion. Plath is shown as too bound up in her own drama to let this woman in. The circle has tightened.

Hughes' treatment of this episode illustrates his poetic skill with narrative. The splitting of each short sentence or phrase by a line ending is a distinct feature of *Birthday Letters*. New sentences suddenly swing open in the middle of a line, carry us through to the next, then stop just as another one opens. This constant jumping-forward not only creates momentum, it keeps our eye and attention ready and focused. An unstoppable drama evolves in unstoppable verse. 'But you/Went on writing your postcards.' This momentum picks up ordinary details, makes them dramatic, locates us in a world rich in sharp reality-effects. At times Hughes stands aside from the main drama to show us, as in the gypsy sequence, other sites of relevance and being. Amazing poems emerge, like 'Daffodils'. But. like the passage above, whatever their subject poem after poem ends with an image of tombs, crypts, graves.

Places

Birthday Letters is also a travelogue. Rich in settings and in the sense of place, it begins in London, shows Sylvia reciting Chaucer to cows in the meadows of Grantchester near Cambridge, moves to London again – their wedding – then to their honeymoon in Spain. ('You Hated Spain') . Titles of poems accumulate like the addresses of the itinerants: '18 Rugby Street … 55 Eltisley … 9, Willow Street …', along with others: 'Wuthering Heights … Grand Canyon'. Soon after their trip to the continent suddenly they are in America. 'Chipmunks' announces this somewhat obliquely. A long stay in and around Boston brought Sylvia back to her home regions – the sea 'off beautiful Nauset', the setting of many of the poems in *The Colossus*, her first book. Readers of Hughes' books before *Birthday Letters*, almost his entire life's work, couldn't have known – from his poems – that he had ever lived in America, and not only lived there but travelled extensively through the canyon regions of the South West. With the exception of Moortown, Hughes' method up to the writing of *Birthday Letters* had been to avoid making overt and advertised reference to his private experience, in whole poems at least. America appears, if at all, in the myths and fables of Crow, and then only as narratives derived from Native American folk-tales. One reason for this deliberate omission of any direct reference to America, particularly to America as a place in his published work, could have been its close association with Plath, his marriage, its difficulties and its outcome.

Birthday Letters was biding its time, waiting, as books do, for the right moment, and the American poems certainly make more sense in the book as it is – deeply introspective, and finished during the final year of his life.

His attitude to America (what can anyone's 'attitude' be to America?) must have been coloured by personal troubles difficult to locate in the place itself. 'Fishing Bridge' for example makes some attempts to describe a place:

> What I remember
> Is the sun's dazzle – and your delight
> Wandering off along the lake's fringe
> Towards the shag-headed wilderness
> In your bikini. (BL 87)

A rather bathetic and inconclusive picture, not Hughes at his best. In lines that follow he hits on the image of America as a series of thresholds: 'Every one of them a glittering offer' an image which recurs also in 'Flounders'. Whatever these offers were, neither poet was sure of their direction. The drama, in their real life, was stalling. Their poems too may have been intermittent. Sylvia taught undergraduates at Smith. Hughes' inspiration in *Lupercal* (the poems he was writing at that time) had attached itself firmly to England. The mood was one of searching for a focus not quite found, or not found at least in these environs. When an inkling does occur it seems in excess of the place, out of gear with the described setting. Observing Sylvia's panic in '59th Bear', a poem about a bear stalking a campground, the emphasis as in 'The Table' confesses to missed understanding. Only much later can he supply them. The bear has, in retrospect become a metaphor – 'How the death, hurtling to and fro / inside your head… had to be kept moving.'

But at the time, this particular reading of the scene was out of focus, had to be so, couldn't quite be located. And in 'Fishing Bridge' instead of a signifying place, in sharp perspective, a remarkable passage does occur but decoupled from its immediate geography:

> too many thresholds –

> Each one of them a glittering offer.
> We half-closed our eyes. Or held them wide
> Like sleepwalkers while a voice on a tape,
> Promising, directed us to a doorway
> Difficult and dark. The voice urged on
> Into an unlit maze of crying and loss.
> What voice? 'Find your souls' said the voice.
> 'Find your true selves. This way. Search, search.'
> The voice had never heard of the shining lake.
> 'Find the core of the labyrinth.' Why? What opens
> At the heart of the maze? Is it the doorway
> Into the perfected vision? Masterfully
> The voice pushed us, hypnotised, bowing our heads
> Into its dead-ends, its reversals,
> Dreamy gropings, baffled ponderings,
> Its monomaniac half-search, half-struggle,
> Not for the future – not for any future – (BL 88)

A maze, a doorway, a tape, a voice – but ignoring the shining lake. No focus. We might be grateful for Hughes' honesty here. He doesn't pretend there is one when there isn't. But the writing, powerful and accurate as it may be, lacks that quality of drama that attends his sudden glimpse of Sylvia's face, or the face of the gypsy woman in Rheims. And so America goes missing, even from the poems written about it.

In its place is another drama not yet revealed to Hughes or even to Plath. There are exceptions – 'Carlsbad Caverns'. But even in 'Grand Canyon' a sense of confusion overtakes Hughes' usually direct, descriptive-focusing power. The most successfully focused and therefore dramatised poem in this group, 'The Badlands', flickers across the continent then comes to rest in the Theodore Roosevelt National Park: 'A land with maybe one idea – snake.' Events happen, but there is a sense of deep, predatory upheaval and revelation: 'Empty, horrible, archaic – America / Planetary – before the eye had touched it.' (BL 84)

All this is being seen through the eyes of Plath, and transcribed in chunks into Hughes' voice – that incipient fear of the archaic, and with it a sympathy for the fear. Seeing America through this gaze of fear was her way. He seems too married to see it himself distinctly. She held on to another image of America – the East coast of her grandmother's house near Point Shirley. Her grandmother's telephone number – Ocean 1212W – became the title of the descriptive essay she wrote about this specially remembered place by the Atlantic, the essay later admired by Marianne Moore: 'so wonderful, so lit.'

America, then back to England again. But in between is a poem that could belong to either of these places, and situated right in the middle of the book: 'Black Coat'. All we hear is 'the North Shore ice wind', Hughes wanting to get away, be alone. 'That horizon-wide wipe/Might be a whole new start.' But then he imagines that Sylvia is watching: a 'paparazzo sniper'. All she sees is a man on the beach in the distance – her husband. Then she sees something else – a double image. 'The body of the ghost and me the blurred see-through/Came into single focus.' Now at his feet is 'that freezing sea/From which your dead father had just crawled.' In Plath's gaze, or in Hughes' envisioning of her gaze, 'He slid into me.' And so the return to England has that in mind – in the minds of the readers of *Birthday Letters*. Was it in the minds of its protagonists? It hardly matters. Whatever happens after this point only serves to reinforce the drama of this event, marking a shift in the book's poetic focus. A new and disturbing character had entered. And a new way of writing about people. Something has happened now to the means of seeing. Who you are is not who you think you are, nor is it clear who is looking at what or through whose eyes.

In September 1961 the Hughes's settle in Devon. It is now that the circle begins to tighten irrecoverably. Sights merge. Hughes forgets the source of his own inspiration, gives himself up to hers. There are battles during which he half-realises his sacrifice – as in 'The Rabbit Catcher'. This poem was already a literary subject. Plath's of that title may have been inspired by a poem by Lawrence, 'Love on the Farm'. Hughes attributes it to an experience, narrates it. Was it Hughes or Lawrence Plath was attacking when she describes 'these tight wires between us'? Another woman, Assia Gutman, appears on the Devon stage. And the same woman or maybe another, appears in the poem 'The Pan'. But these women are last attempt escape-routes from the

narrowing circle of Sylvia's downward drive – towards her father and
helplessly focused there, dragging Hughes with her.

But Devon had been an assertion of his need. 'I brought you to
Devon. I brought you into my dreamland./I sleepwalked you/ Into
my land of totems. Never-never land:/ The orchard in the West.'
Only to ask 'What wrong fork/Had we taken?' To most of us now a
Devon cottage, sprawling with thatch, could seem a kind of idyll.
But to Sylvia it wasn't. 'The world/Came to an end at bullocks/
Huddled behind gates, knee-deep in quag.' Again he is seeing it
through her eyes, as maybe an Alpha-achieving American would see
it. He has the misfortune to take her to Woolacombe Beach, imagining
this will somehow restore her spirits by reminding her of her long-
loved ocean. She refused to get out of the car. Hughes sums up her
American view of England, England at the start of the 1960s: 'London
a morgue of dinge – English dinge./Our sole indigenous art-form –
depressionist!'

The impulse behind the Woolacombe trip and other similar
attempts by Hughes is clear – it was to get her to focus, but on
something other than the developing psychic catastrophe that was
beginning in Devon. Was her descent inexorable? Were there other
directions for her poetry? Hughes speaks of 'An Avalon for which I
had the wavelength' – 'my land of totems'. He hopes to deflect Plath
from the track to disaster, 'to set inside your head another jewel'. He
hopes the sea will administer to her 'the gentlest electric shock', but
this line hardly by accident recalls, even as it is spoken, the actual
shock treatment that had scarred her forehead in her teens – a
corrective considerably more violent. His hopes came to nothing.
No such instructions could be received from Devon. Or, if there
were, these came with a bleakness and beauty captured by Plath in
her poem 'The Moon and the Yew Tree' from *Ariel*.

Endings

Of 'The Moon and the Yew Tree' Hughes comments: 'It depressed
me greatly. It's my suspicion that no poem can be a poem that is not
a statement from the powers in control of our life, the ultimate
suffering and decision in us.' (ASP pp 81-88) He had shown her a

scene from one of the windows of their house just before dawn. When he returned at the end of that day she had written it. This was Hughes as tutor again, but deeply alarmed by the force that had been unleashed. As a book about the creative process, *Birthday Letters* moves through a series of phases, charting the course of Plath's search for directives, instructions, commands, for that focus which would allow her to see in her own life the shape of a myth. If we accept his narrative of this process, it's clear that his own position towards it bore shades of ambivalence: admiration perhaps but mostly shock. Acting as guide he became a reluctant guide and finally helpless. Also, a degree of sacrifice of his own inspirational sources was involved. They stayed at the edge of the vortex which Plath entered.

A vortex and a whirlwind. 'His roar was like a basement furnace/ Thunder in the foundations.' ('The God'). The only directive for Plath was to descend, to burn in the flames that explode on the jacket cover of *Birthday Letters*. But this was not to become Hughes' God. Some time before the end of their marriage, his and Plath's wavelengths had separated. Her poems, however, implicated him, and just as her poem 'Daddy' from Ariel sees her father and Hughes as one person, so Hughes in poems at the end of *Birthday Letters* recognised the fate of this figure in the drama. The wounded father in his poem 'The Cast' could be the wounded Hughes. Years of humiliation for him followed the publication of *Ariel* with its images of fascism, German brutalism, male violence towards women and Jews. In the story Plath discovered in *Ariel*, the father had to be killed, 'staked', like a vampire, Hughes with him.

'The Gypsy' and a related poem set in London, 'Epiphany', where Hughes is offered a fox-cub for a pound but rejects the offer, dramatise how during even the more stable periods of their relationship this marriage of creative minds was being sustained at some cost to his own poetic resources. It is a paradox, perhaps an irony, that at the end of his life this story of how they were temporarily put to one side should bring them at last to such powerful realisation. It was only through his *not* being trapped in the vortex this could occur. The opposite impulse leads upward and outward, evolves towards a widening of the world. Yet there is great tenderness for Plath in this book, not least in the final poem 'Red', the red of flames, blood, violence and pain. The final line of the book stands on its own, and recalls that 'jewel in your head' – the miles of Nauset surf, one of Plath's sources of earlier inspiration. Red yes. In the end, red for all it was worth. 'But the jewel you lost was blue.'

REFERENCES
BL: Ted Hughes, *Birthday Letters*, Faber 1998
Also: *Lupercal*, Faber 1962; *Crow*, Faber 1972

ASP: Ted Hughes: 'The Chronological Order of Sylvia Plath's Poems', *The Art of Sylvia Plath* (ed. Charles Newman), Faber 1970

GLOSSARY

This Glossary is intended to help the reader who comes across a term or reference that is unfamiliar. Given the range of approaches in this book, it would not be surprising for at least some of the terminology to be unfamiliar to many readers. The definitions are not detailed, and in some cases refer to the particular use made of a term in these pages.

affect: Used here it means the emotional value that a text may have. The power to move the reader.

abjection: A Kristevan concept referring to the 'outsider' status of some groups of people, including women.

androgyny, androgynous: In this context, these words refer to writers whose gender does not influence their outlook, or who are deliberately 'ungendered' in their writing.

anthropomorphic: The practice of attributing human characteristics to animals. This may include physical characteristics, such as the wearing of clothes, and psychological ones such as friendship or sadness.

avant la lettre: French expression used in English to refer to things that anticipate a term to name them. Any literary fashion or movement may therefore have examples which predate the naming of the trend.

Bakhtin: Critical theorist known for his view that literature 'makes new' the things it describes. Also known for calling literature 'dialogic' and 'heretoglossic' (qv).

blank verse: Verse which is written in *unrhymed* iambic pentameter. Common in Shakespeare, particularly the tragedies. Not to be confused with free verse (which does not conform to any regular metre).

Chomsky: A linguist and political commentator, influential in linguistic theory in the mid-to-late 20th century. He proposed models of grammar which depended on the metaphor of language-as-machine, rather than the earlier language-as-store cupboard metaphor. His ideas were developed by introspection first and tested against data later.

closure: In this context, closure refers to the 'clinching' or resolution of a poem's meaning, particularly at the end e.g. the last two lines of traditional sonnets. Not all poems have closure, and it is often seen as a virtue in recent times for poems to avoid such a restriction on their meaning.

coding time, content time, receiving time: These terms refer to the different time zones recognisable in the production and reception of a linguistic message. The coding and receiving time might be the same, though writing and recording of speech make them theoretically separate. Content time is the time zone represented in the text itself, and this may be variable.

cognitive processing: The mental activity during which language (in this context) is produced and/or understood.

commodify: The process by which things which are not obviously commercial (such as education, bodies, ideas) are nevertheless made into commodities with potential for trading. Here used to describe the burgeoning commercialisation of printing and publishing of texts.

conceit: an unusually far-fetched or elaborate metaphor or simile, drawing parallels between two apparently dissimilar things.

connotations, negative/positive: The associations a word has, which are not part of its denotative meaning, e.g., 'father' means 'male parent' but connotes love and protection. Very often connotations are negative or positive in their force, though they might quite neutrally suggest associations with groups of people (e.g. 'tummy' connotes children) or places (e.g. 'the accused' connotes legal courts).

conversation analysis: A sub-branch of sociolinguistics, influenced by anthropology, which investigates the patterns inherent in conversation, particularly casual everyday conversation.

corpus lexicology: Lexicology is the study of words and word meanings and is at the basis of much dictionary-making (lexicography). Though traditional dictionaries were based on literary or elevated usage of words, corpus lexicology underlies much of modern dictionary making and relies for evidence of word usage on a large body of material, often spoken as well as written and usually stored on computer.

couplet: Two lines of poetry linked together, usually by end-rhymes, but possibly also by layout or other formal features.

decasyllables: Lines of poetry 10 syllables long (and see syllabics, below).

declarative sentences: Sentences which make a statement, rather than asking a question, giving an instruction etc.

definite article: In English the definite article is 'the'.

definite referring expressions: In English other definite referring expressions include those using demonstratives such as 'this', 'these', 'that' and 'those' as well as possessives such as 'his' or 'your'.

deixis: Some aspects of human language have shifting reference, depending on the identity and positioning of the speaker or writer. These are known as deictic features and the phenomenon of shifting reference (or point of view) is known as deixis.

demonstrative determiners: The words 'this', 'these', 'that' and 'those', when used in front of a noun, are called demonstrative determiners. They are interchangeable with other determiners, such as definite articles (q.v.), but give more specific (deictic) information than articles.

demonstrative pronouns: The words 'this', 'these', 'that' and 'those', when used as a complete noun phrase in themselves, are known as demonstrative pronouns. For example, in the sentence: 'These are my favourite shoes', the word 'these' acts alone as the subject of the sentence.

dialogical: Bakhtin was responsible for articulating this version of the idea that all texts are dialogic in the sense that they enter into 'dialogues' with other texts, both in their immediate and in the wider (including historical) context.

discourse: Usually means to include more than mere words and structures in its scope, e.g., a particular kind of language used by certain groups or in certain settings (e.g. classroom discourse); or the kind of language that helps to 'construct' reality by its ways of categorising and conceptualising aspects of the world (e.g. patriarchal discourse) or simply used to indicate that the participants, their background, experience and relationships are all included (as in the phrase 'discourse analysis').

first/second person pronouns: In English, the first person pronouns are 'I', 'me', 'we' and 'us'. The second person pronoun is 'you'.

fixed collocation: 'Collocation' refers to the combination of words that occur in a language. Many are freely made by the speakers, but there are some that are either 'restricted' (i.e. there are few options) or are completely fixed (i.e. there is no option). Idioms such as 'How do you do?' are usually fixed collocations.

generic sentences: This term refers to sentences that make generalised comments about the world, rather than referring specifically to participants or actions in the context. The most famous one in English literature is probably the opening sentence of Jane Austen's *Pride and Prejudice*: 'It is a truth universally acknowledged, that a single man in possession of a good fortune, must be in want of a wife.'

genre: Denotes a classification of texts into groupings which share some aspects of their form and/or their style and often also their content or subject-matter, e.g., 'novel', 'play', 'poem' and more specifically 'detective novel', 'radio drama', 'lyric poem'.

half-rhyme: Imperfect rhyme, where the consonants agree, but the vowel sounds don't, or vice versa: e.g. 'tent/slant'; 'bath/laugh'.

heteroglossic: Refers to the 'many-tongued' nature of much literature, which is thus designated as having a range of potential viewpoints, rather than the traditional notion of texts being the mouthpiece of the author. First used by Bakhtin.

honorifics: A general term to refer to the kinds of titles used to different groups of people according to status in a society. Thus Professor, Dr, Mr, Ms etc. would qualify as honorifics in British (and some other English speaking) societies.

iambic pentameter: A line or lines of five iambic feet; i.e. poetry written in lines of nine, ten or eleven syllables and using an alternating unstressed and stressed rhythm.

internal rhyme: Words rhyme within the body of the line, rather than at the ends of the line.

intertextual reference: A direct allusion to other texts, usually expected to be known by the reader, though not always in practice. Intertextuality more generally refers to the tendency for texts to allude to each other indirectly or even unconsciously through their common cultural or historical bases.

Kristeva: Lacanian theorist who takes a particularly feminist slant on the psychoanalytical development of children and who emphasises the female potential for keeping in touch with the anarchic semiotic (qv) symbolism that is a feature of pre-linguistic development.

Labov: Labov is a sociolinguist renowned for his work on inner-city social dialects in New York and for his pioneering methodologies which made casual conversation more accessible to the researcher.

Lacan: Psychologist and theorist whose development of Freudian analysis included the Imaginary (qv) and the Symbolic (qv).

magic realism: A sub-genre of novel-writing, popular toward the end of the twentieth century and particularly in post-colonial settings. It combines realistic narrative with fantastic and/or supernatural occurrences.

matrilineage: The handing down of traditions (including names), and often wealth, by the female, rather than the more common male, line.

Meredithian sonnet: Sixteen line sonnet, following the example of George Meredith's Victorian sonnet-sequence.

minimalism: A style based on the extreme restriction of a work's contents to a bare minimum of necessary elements.

modality: The technique whereby texts demonstrate the opinion of the author (or implied author) toward the content of the text. These include modal verbs (e.g. 'might', 'shall', 'could') as well as adverbs ('possibly', 'maybe') and other word classes (e.g. verb: 'think' and adjective: 'probable'). **epistemic modality:** The opinion of the author as to the text's likely truth is demonstrated by epistemic modals (e.g. '*Surely* he won't come late again?'). **deontic modality:** These modals refer to the author's opinion of the desirability (or otherwise) of a text's content (e.g. 'I *wish* she'd talk a bit louder').

naturalisation, naturalised: The process by which opinions, attitudes and ideas become part of the 'common sense' current in a particular society or sub-social group. It normally also recognises the part that language and texts play in this process. These ideas and opinions become so basic to the social outlook that they are perceived as the 'truth'.

performance: In linguistic contexts, this term usually refers to the messy reality of everyday language use, as opposed to the apparently neat systems and structures that appear in dictionaries and grammar books and possibly also in our brains.

poetics: The general principles of poetry or the theoretical study of these principles.

point of view: The vantage point from which a text is presenting the scene and actions it describes. It may shift within a passage or remain constant.

polysemy: The multiple meaning of words, very common in English, whereby a word's senses are related to each other by meaning, but different enough to warrant separate definition. For example, the word 'run' has at least the following related ('polysemous') senses: propel yourself quickly over the ground, organise (run a company), make work (run a machine), merge (colours, dyes), ladder (stockings).

postmodern, -ism: Following on from, and often opposed to, modernism. A late twentieth century approach to art typically ironic and self-referential.

pragmatics: The study of textual meaning, taking contextual information into account. Pragmatics concerns itself with the kinds of processing that must take place when human beings use language in real settings.

psycholinguistics: Branch of linguistics concerned with the psychological aspects of language learning and use. Most commonly studying how children learn to speak and modelling the language of people with different kinds of speech and language difficulty.

quatrain: Four line stanza (or verse).

register: The kind of language (often distinguished by style and/or specialised vocabulary) that is used in a particular context or by a group of people with shared interests, e.g., the language of mining, PR, knitting, hotel catering etc.

reification: Literally referring to the conversion of a person or abstract concept into a thing, this term is often used when something that is intangible and has vague boundaries is nevertheless treated as a recognisable, and often, but not always, revered entity.

Semiotic: The particular use of Semiotic here refers to Kristeva's conceptualising of the pre-linguistic meanings that infants have access to, but which are often suppressed after the onset of language, or 'entry into the Symbolic order' in Lacanian terms.

sibilants: A subset of the speech sounds known as fricatives. They include /s/ and /z/ in English and have a 'grooved' tongue making the sound more focused and 'whistling' than the more messy non-sibilants such as /f/ and /v/.

sociolinguistics: A branch of linguistics that researches into the interface between society and linguistic variety and focuses on social dialects.

spatial adverbs: Adverbs of place such as 'there', 'somewhere', 'here', 'nearby' etc.

speech and thought representation: The way in which people's words and thoughts are conveyed by texts.

subjectivity: This use of the term indicates the extent to which people construct their own identities as 'subjects', i.e., as active participants in their fate rather than as 'objects' or passive sufferers of fate.

surreal: Refers to an artistic movement of the beginning of the 20th century, Surrealism, which began the move away from naturalistic representation by drawing on unlikely combinations of reality.

syllabic: Lines of verse measured merely by the number of syllables, rather than stressed and unstressed syllables.

Symbolic: Refers In this context to the stage of development at which children enter into language and thus begin to operate through the 'reality' that their language constructs for them. Used by Lacan and Kristeva.

temporal adverbs: Adverbs of time, e.g., 'then', 'now', 'eventually', 'later' etc.

tense: English verbs are complex, but only have two genuine tenses – present and past. We manage to convey the future using modal verbs ('will see') and the recent finished or unfinished past using combinations of progressive and perfective auxiliary verbs such as in 'having eaten' or 'has been singing'.

textworld: The idea of textworlds is that the reader gradually builds a picture of what the world inside the text is like. There is much discussion as to how varied different readers' textworlds of a single text will be.

transitivity: The choice of a verb not only to convey an action, but to represent it in a way that emphasises some aspect of the situation, such as the active or willing initiator or the passive recipient. 'John hit Bill' emphasises John's action whereas 'Bill was hurt' emphasises the result.

vocatives: Names as called out to attract their owners' attention.